THE LIBRARY
ST. MARY'S COLLEGE OF MARYLAND
ST. MARY'S CITY, MARYLAND 20686

Desire and Deligh

DESIRE AND DELIGHT

A New Reading of Augustine's *Confessions*

Margaret R. Miles

CROSSROAD · NEW YORK

For Owen, Janet, and Richard

1992

The Crossroad Publishing Company
370 Lexington Avenue, New York, NY 10017

Copyright © 1991 Lindau S.r.l.

All rights reserved. No part of this book may be reproduced,
stored in a retrieval system, or transmitted, in any form
or by any means, electronic, mechanical, photocopying,
recording, or otherwise, without the written permission of
The Crossroad Publishing Company.

Printed in the United States of America

Library of Congress Cataloging-in-Publication Data

Miles, Margaret Ruth.
    Desire and delight : a new reading of Augustine's Confessions /
Margaret R. Miles.
        p.   cm.
    ISBN 0-8245-1163-8
    1. Augustine, Saint, Bishop of Hippo.   Confessiones.   I. Title.
BR65.A62M55   1992
242—dc20   92-13329
                                                            CIP

Contents

Preface

inardescimus et imus[1]

Perhaps it should be acknowledged at the outset that my most recent reading of Augustine's *Confessions*—as a text of pleasure—was influenced by the way I read it. Let me explain. Almost a decade and a half ago I studied Augustine passionately. I wrote my doctoral dissertation on his idea of the meaning and value of the human body. Since then, however, I have reread Augustine only in pieces, in pressured preparation for classes and seminars. Those later readings produced an Augustine which, in his own words, was "a piece of difficult ground, not to be worked over without much sweat" (X.16). In the summer of 1989, however, I planned a markedly different reading experience than those frenzied and problematizing readings in preparation for teaching a class. I went with three dear friends for a month to the blue-and-white Greek island of Paros, taking with me the *Confessions* in Latin. In the mornings I read Augustine excitedly, making copious notes, examining Augustine's language and grammar in detail. Afternoons, we went to a beach where I

7

sat under a tree and pondered the morning's reading, sometimes writing pages of ideas I had about it, sometimes writing nothing, but letting ideas float in and out like the softly lapping Mediterranean—the same sea that touched Ostia and Hippo Regius. Evenings were for eating, drinking, and talking. Then we walked home in the warm darkness, along the wharf, under the large sky polka-dotted with stars. I had hoped to find that I did not think well under conditions of such pleasure and luxury, but this was not my experience.

It will be up to the reader to evaluate the reading of the *Confessions* generated by the circumstances I have described. The experience itself reminded me of why I became an academic in the first place. It was for the pleasure of the kind of passionate engagement with books and ideas that I again experienced on the island of Paros. My own pleasure alerted me to an aspect of the *Confessions* I had not noticed when I read it as an anxious doctoral student or, subsequently, as a harried teacher.

My earlier readings were not wrong. Augustine's astoundingly accurate description of *concupiscentia* as a repetition compulsion, a frantic pursuit of frustratingly elusive pleasure, does reveal the totalitarian scope of his anxiety.[2] His tortured efforts to gather a philosophical basis for establishing a Christian anthropology *are* a prominent feature of the *Confessions*.[3] His interest in asceticism as a method for maintaining the vividness and freshness of the Christian life,[4] his search for a style of dealing with other human beings not characterized by "eating one another up, as people do with their food,"[5] a style he will come to call "loving the neighbor in God"[6]: these and other interests accurately characterize Augustine's authorship. Yet I now understand each of them to be aspects of an interest even more consuming and ardent, that of analyzing how to get—and keep—the greatest degree of pleasure.

The "reading" of the *Confessions* I offer here is not designed to replace my reader's own reading of the *Confessions*. I will assume familiarity with Augustine's text throughout, and will point out some of its features that seem most vivid and unique to me. Optimally, my reading might inspire you to reread the *Confessions*. The *Confessions* deserves to be called a great piece of literature in that it repays an almost infinite number of readings. In Augustine's colorful Latin, the *Confessions* is overwhelming; it is next to impossible to maintain a stance of critical detachment. Even in translation, the beauty and richness of Augustine's language, his passion and honesty, and the powerful resolution of his search for "God and the self" are evident. The reader is quickly seduced into passionate relationship—sometimes violent disagreement, sometimes frustration, sometimes amazement that a North African who lived over fifteen hundred years ago could express so accurately an idea or emotion one recognizes so intimately. Reading the *Confessions* is a pleasure; this is perhaps the most straightforward meaning of my claim that it is a text of pleasure.

Yet pleasure is culturally constructed; it is particular, not universal. What gave the author and his first audience pleasure may not pleasure a reader almost fifteen hundred years distant in time. Readers, like lovers, are sensitized to particular beauties and blind to others. On what basis, then, can it be asserted without qualification that the *Confessions* is a pleasurable text? Chapters 1 and 2 will examine the multiple meanings of this assertion, not in order to demonstrate exhaustively "the pleasure of the text,"[7] but in order to stimulate the reader's recognition of the complexity of textual pleasure. Because textual pleasure is achieved by particular strategies that can be detected and analyzed, I will examine the devices by which Augustine endeavors to maintain the reader's emotional and intellectual engagement with his text—surely the first requirement for a pleasurable text. How, I will ask, do the *Confessions* produce in the reader a responsive kaleidoscope of feeling—gratification, denial, frustration, discomfort, and satisfaction?

According to Augustine, hermeneutics—the art of interpretation—is not a problem for the angels, who have "no need of reading to understand [God's] word":

> They read without syllables that are spoken in time. . . . They read; they choose; they love; their reading is perpetual, and what they read never passes away. . . . Their book is never closed, for you yourself are their book. (XIII.15)

Human beings, however, do not grasp either God's or each other's self-revelations with this immediacy. They do not read what is written, for reading is, inevitably and irreducibly, interpretation.

I therefore recognize the necessity of analyzing my side of the conversation I have had with Augustine's text. My sensitivities are different from Augustine's; different experiences inform and activate them. Some of these differences are obvious: difference in time and space is the most prominent. Race, gender, and class differences also inform—sometimes frustrate—my pleasure in reading. As an obedient reader I have endeavored to grasp what Augustine worked to communicate. As a disobedient reader, I have allowed my sensitivities to highlight features of the *Confessions* that Augustine considered accidental or incidental to his self-revelation, finding these asides, bits of information, attitudes, and assumptions more revealing than Augustine might have wished them to be.

Reading Augustine's *Confessions* requires that one must somehow manage to see simultaneously the problems and dangers of Augustine's thought—the authoritarianism, the exclusionary strategies—*and* its extraordinary power and beauty. If one sees only the former, the popularity and influence of the *Confessions* will continue to puzzle. Moreover, to insist on seeing only the horrors is to imagine generation after generation of credulous readers who permitted themselves to be bullied by the text, jockeyed into positions of helpless and passive voyeurism and acquiescence. One must imagine readers who were willing to exchange for their critical faculties the mild titillation of Augustine's lifestory—cheap thrills, indeed! This interpretive stance fails to respect the myriad readers who found the *Confessions* a poignant, gripping, and transformative text.

On the other hand, if one reads in the *Confessions* only its powerful beauty, one is susceptible to its many seductions, its prohibitions, its silences, its politics, and institutional allegiences. A text—any text, but especially a powerful text—not only reflects but also contributes to the reproduction of the social arrangements it assumes, supports, or advocates. Its values and loyalties, then, must be examined, problematized, and their social and institutional effects noticed. Influential texts are not, of course, all-powerful, and the "great ideas" approach to explaining why the world is as it is, and people act as they do, is a methodological fallacy perpetrated by intellectuals. Nevertheless, the influence of the *Confessions*, its role in forming Western institutions—like monasticism, church, and marriage—cannot be overestimated. What is subordinated in the *Confessions* has largely been undervalued also in Western culture—for example, women and the natural world of bodies and senses. It cannot be claimed that the *Confessions caused* such marginalizations, but neither can it be doubted that the *Confessions* contributed to the shaping of Western values, social arrangements, and institutions.

An adequate reading of the *Confessions*, then, must demonstrate both its strong beauty and its politics because both speak simultaneously. You get the cultural message, Roland Barthes once said, in the same instant that you get the pleasure. The pleasure of the text carries and coats the message; the greater the pleasure, the more effectively and directly is the message transported. A careful and thorough inspection of text, context, and subtext will reveal a fine network of intended and unintended effects. Given the limitations of discursive language, however, no explication can demonstrate both simultaneously. While we are entranced, we are not usually critical. And so a sort of interpretive cyclic oscillation must occur in which strands separated for close examination are gathered and rewoven. Necessarily discussed seriatim, text, context, and subtext must subsequently be mixed, as the separate instruments on different soundtracks are mixed, if the music of the text is to be heard in its full strength and beauty.

Augustine was well aware of—and frightened by—the unpredictablity and volatility of interpretation. He remarked with bravado, "Let proud-hearted men laugh at me, and those who have not yet, for their own health, been struck down and crushed by you, my God" (IV.1); yet his parents' laughter at the dreaded punishments of his childhood schoolmasters still haunted the middle-aged Augustine (I.9). He was terrified of being laughed at, and repeatedly specifies his imagined reader as one who *will not laugh*. Conscious of readers' possible reactions, he attempts to direct those reactions toward gentle indulgence:

> I know that your spiritual ones will be smiling at me, though kindly and lovingly, if they read the story of these confusions of mind. (V.10)

Given his fear of derisive laughter, it is also a measure of Augustine's greatness that in spite of fearing misunderstanding, misinterpretation, and misrepresentation, he purposely wrote in a way that invited multiple interpretations:

> I prefer to write in such a way that my words could convey any truth that anyone could grasp on such matters, rather than to set down one true meaning so clearly as to exclude all other meanings which, not being false, could not offend me. (XII.31)

The problem of interpretation is anticipated by the problem of expression. How is Augustine to describe what he most wants to describe—the movements of the soul? Aristotle had written: "The soul's passions all seem to be linked with a body, as the body undergoes modifications in their presence." [8] Thus, ironically, if he is accurately to represent the soul's process, Augustine must rigorously observe the body's movements—its reactions and responses. His vehicle for characterizing inner movement is physical change. His remarkable ability to find the most vivid—even violent—metaphor is at its peak in his use of the body as symbol and site of subjectivity. He writes, for example, of the fevers, swellings, wounds, and scabs of his youthful lust; he describes a sort of *anorexia nervosa* of the soul:

> I was starved inside me for inner food . . . yet this starvation did not make me hungry. I had no desire for the food that is incorruptible, and this was not because I was filled with it; no, the more I was famished for lack of it, the more my stomach turned against it. (III.1)

Because the soul's fluctuations are discernible only as physical events, the body must be painstakingly scrutinized for knowledge of the soul. Augustine's detailed interest in the body—his own body—makes the *Confessions* a profoundly erotic text. Chapter 3 will endeavor to show that the eroticism of the *Confessions* is not confined to the recounting of erotic experience; Augustine's variable and polymorphous *eros* permeates and structures the text. His model of pleasure was informed by his experience of sexual pleasure, and male sexuality, with its rhythm of collecting and spilling provides Augustine's template for spiritual pleasure.

Chapter 4 will discuss Augustine's world, seen from the perspective of the converted eye, as described in books 10 to 13 of the *Confessions*. Here a different, reconstructed pleasure prevails. Having lived to the bitter end of the agenda of concupiscence, and experienced to the full its debilitating effects, Augustine has found the relief and freedom of what he now considers "true pleasure." Yet, curiously, the new pleasure of the converted Augustine fails to produce a descriptive text as engrossing as that of his misspent youth. Augustine's passion, intensity, and eroticism are not missing from these books, but they are less evident, more invested in a vision of an orderly universe.

For the news—"so old and so new" (X. 27)—of the *Confessions* is that beauty is not, to the naked eye, beautiful. The powerful, perverse beauty of the twisted psyche seeking light and nourishment is revealed only after a relaxation of this anxious grasping. Only then can one see that each object, person, and event is good; together, the whole is very good, and—more to the point of the *Confessions*—"to perceive all the parts together at once would give more pleasure than to perceive each individual part separately" (IV.11). In the meantime, however, the loud urgency of the longing flesh conceals the design, the composition, in which *all of it* will have a place, a part to play, in which nothing will be lost.

> And we, who have always thought
> of happiness as rising, would feel the emotion
> that almost startles
> when happiness falls.[9]

1

The Search for Pleasure: "Disorder and Early Sorrow"[10]

When Augustine was a young teacher of rhetoric in the imperial capital of Milan, he saw one day on the street a poor but happy beggar. The beggar's drunken happiness contrasted sharply with Augustine's unhappiness. Augustine, panting "for honors, for money, for marriage," and worried about a speech that he was soon to deliver in praise of the emperor, envied the beggar his carefree, if temporary, happiness. Telling the story a decade later, he interpreted it in a way that would not have occurred to him at the time:

> I found bitterness and difficulty in following these desires, and your graciousness to me was shown in the

way you would not allow me to find anything sweet
which was not you. . . . How unhappy [my soul] was
then! And you pricked its wound on the quick so that
it might leave everything else and turn to you . . . I
was unhappy indeed, and you made me really see my
unhappiness. (VI.6)

The beggar "fairly drunk, I suppose, was laughing
and enjoying himself," a sight which depressed Augustine. He reflected that all his strenuous efforts to
secure the success that would make him happy had
failed to reach even the temporary state of happiness
the beggar enjoyed: "he was happy while I was unhappy; he was carefree while I was full of fears." Profes-
sionally oriented to pleasing others by his speeches,
Augustine cannot pleasure himself: "I got no joy out of
my learning. Instead I used it to give pleasure to men."
Although Augustine tried to console himself by re-
flecting on the brevity of the beggar's joy—"the beggar
would sleep off his drunkenness that very night"—Augustine had to acknowledge that his own "drunkenness" was never alleviated: "I had gone to bed with mine
and woken up with it day after day after day and I
would go on doing so."

In describing the incident, Augustine corrects his
earlier feeling of envy: "the beggar's joy was not true joy
. . . certainly it makes a difference what is the source
of a man's happiness." Yet the recognition of his own
unhappiness remains the essential core of the story.

I was eaten up with anxieties . . . things were not at all
well with me, and I worried about it, and by worrying
made matters twice as bad, and if fortune seemed to
smile on me at all, I felt too tired to grasp my opportunity. (VI.6)

The forty-year-old Augustine, bishop of Hippo, was still, like the thirty-year-old "yuppie," fascinated by the mystery of human happiness. What pleasures contributed to happiness? Which could guarantee its permanence? How was the greatest happiness to be secured?

The *Confessions* is *about* pleasure; it is a detailed introspection of human happiness. It seeks to answer the questions posed in the preceeding paragraph by narrating Augustine's experiential/experimental search for powerful and permanent pleasure. In this chapter we will follow Augustine's inspection of pleasure as it organizes the narrative of his early life.

The pleasure offered by the *Confessions* is not, however, that of a humorous book. Laughter was, as we have already noted, deeply problematic for Augustine. Laughter, as Augustine understood it, is not innocent, but always at someone's expense. It requires both target and accomplices. The small boy Augustine laughed with his friends at their success in deceiving the owner of a pear tree from which they stole, an act, he says in retrospect, that he would never have done by himself. Inspecting his own enjoyment of the deed, he asks "Why, then, was my pleasure of such a kind that I did not do the act by myself? Was it because people do not generally laugh by themselves?" (II.9)

Laughter can also mask self-deception; the rebellious gang—the Subverters—Augustine participated in as a youth gave themselves "malicious amusement" by mocking and jeering. Yet it was they who were the deceived: "when they took pleasure in mocking and deceiving others, there were hidden within themselves deceiving spirits, laughing at them and leading them

astray" (III.3). Similarly, a joking response to an earnest theological question distresses Augustine: "Personally, I would rather say: 'I don't know,' when I don't
know, than make that kind of a reply which brings
ridicule on someone who has asked a deep question"
(XI.12). Yet he imagines God's laughter as one of the
disciplinary devices by which he was brought to conversion (VI.6,14). And Augustine, who dreaded that
others might laugh at him, makes sure that he has
the final interpretation, the "last laugh": "Anyone who
cannot see [abstract principles] may laugh at me for
talking of them, and, while he laughs, I shall be sorry
for him" (X.12). Clearly, laughter was not a simple pleasure for Augustine, but the symbol and symptom of a
real or an illusory power.

The *Confessions* is, among other things, a narrative deconstruction of what is ordinarily thought of as
pleasurable, and a reconstruction of "true" pleasure.
Augustine's criterion for the adequacy of various orien-
tations and organizations of human life was which
kind of life provides the most intense and lasting pleasure. He was quite clear about what constituted the
condition of greatest pleasure by the time he wrote
the *Confessions*. The *Confessions* narrates his own
process from restlessness, frustration, and irritation
to contentment, equilibrium, a sense of stability,
rightness in the universe, and orientation.

But let us begin at the beginning, as Augustine
did. He was unique in his time in beginning his autobiography with prenatal "experience," if it can be called
that. He entered this world with nothing more than life
and a body, "equipped with senses, fitted with limbs,
adorned with its due proportion, and . . . all the im-

pulses of a living creature" (I.7). The human body is itself a model of order in its complementarity of parts and functions. This complementarity is not limited to one body's integrity, but is social. The infant's first langauge is body language. Augustine marvels at the pre-arranged reciprocity by which an infant's need for milk is matched by a woman's desire to give milk. At this stage in life, pleasure is simple: "all I knew was how to suck, to be content with bodily pleasure, and to be discontented with bodily pain; that was all" (I.6). Is the infant Augustine, though completely absent from the adult Augustine's memory, really connected to him? When do "life and a body" become a self?

The simple needs and satisfactions of early infancy, however, vanish all too soon; frustration occurs. Unable to communicate with precision, the infant discovers a distance between his desires, which are inside him, and those who might have fulfilled them, who are outside him. The result is anger at being thwarted, expressed by jerking limbs, screaming, and tears. Augustine does not shrink from calling this infant anger sin; it is harmless to himself and others only because the infant is powerless to hurt, "not because of innocence of mind" (I.7).

> As it is [adults] put up kindly enough with this behavior, not because there is nothing wrong with it, or nothing much wrong, but because it will disappear as the child grows older. (I.7)

This particular behavior may gradually disappear, but its structure, Augustine finds, remains remarkably constant into adulthood. Already provided for, the infant Augustine "cried for more." Motivated by desire, the young boy Augustine acquired speech in order better to communicate his demands:

> By making all sorts of cries and noises, all sorts of movements of my limbs, I desired to express my inner feelings, so that people would do what I wanted; but I was incapable of expressing everything I desired to express and I was incapable of making everyone understand. Then I turned things over in my memory. When other people gave a particular name to some object and, as they spoke, turned toward this object, I grasped the fact that the sound they uttered was the name given by them to the object which they wished to indicate. That they meant this object and no other one was clear from the movements of their bodies, a kind of universal langauge, expressed by the face, the direction of the eye, gestures of the limbs and tones of the voice, all indicating the state of feeling in the mind as it seeks, enjoys, rejects, or avoids various objects. . . . So I was able to share with those about me in this language for the communication of our desires. (I.8)

In boyhood—which Augustine refuses to call "innocent"—the self was constituted by desires, "a vigorous memory," and language (I.20).

The habit, embedded at an early age, of anxiously grasping objects in the fear that something will be missed, remains the same although the objects change. Augustine says in retrospect: "I looked for pleasures, exaltations, truths not in God himself but in his creatures, and so I fell straight into sorrows, confusions, and mistakes" (I.20). Writing of his boyhood, Augustine identifies the structure of sin as compulsive pursuit of objects, good in themselves, but ultimately unable to satisfy infinite need:

What we liked to do was to play and for this we were punished by those who were themselves behaving in just the same way. But the amusements of older people are called "business," and when children indulge in their own amusements, these older people punish them for it. (I.9)

Augustine sees no need to quibble about differences between the objects of the schoolboy ("footballs, nuts, and pet sparrows"); the businessman ("gold, estates, and slaves"); and the schoolmaster, intent on demonstrating mastery of even the most trifling academic point of argument (I.19).

What may come as a surprise to the careful reader of the *Confessions* is that although Augustine refuses to differentiate between the infant's "sin" of "crying for more," and the businessman's pursuit of gain, he suggests that the appropriate attitude to both should be sympathy rather than judgment: "And no one is sorry for the children; no one is sorry for the older people; no one is sorry for both of them" (I.10). Augustine's autobiography consistently supports his interpretation of the compulsive pursuit and acquisition of objects, not only as lacking pleasure—even in success—but as positively painful. Insomnia is the metaphor Augustine used to describe the affective content of concupiscence:

What tortuous ways these were, and how hopeless was the plight of my foolhardy soul which hoped to have something better if it went away from you! It has turned indeed, over and over, on back and side and front, and always the bed was hard and you alone are rest. (VI.6)

It is true that this interpretation of his childhood and youth leads inexorably to the middle-aged Augustine's claim to have found rest, stability, and equilibrium in God. Perhaps Augustine insists on remembering only the discomfort and anxiety in order to reinforce his middle-aged synthesis. Nevertheless, lacking strong reasons to question an author's reported feeling, it is presumptuous to second-guess what Augustine says he felt.

We can, however, consider Augustine's rhetorical predelictions—his textual strategies—for controlling his reader's reaction to his narration. For example, his preference for black-and-white evaluation of the people and events of his early life can be observed. Augustine's description of his parents' role in his life illustrates his penchant for contrasting people who helped him toward his conversion to Catholic Christianity with those who encouraged him to resist conversion.

Readers of the *Confessions* first meet Patricius, his father, as Patricius spends "more money than his means really allowed" to educate the young Augustine. Rather than acknowledging gratitude, Augustine remarks only that his father was not interested in Augustine's relationship with God or in whether he was chaste, but only in how cultured he was (II.3). The passage contrasts Patricius's pleasure at the signs of Augustine's maturity, seen at a public bath, with his mother's "holy fear and trembling" at Augustine's prospects for sexual activity. Patricius's satisfaction in observing Augustine's body ("his pleasure proceeded from that kind of drunkenness in which the world forgets you, its creator, and falls in love with your creature instead") is juxtaposed to Monica's sober warnings ("Whose words were they except yours which, by means of my mother, your devoted servant, you kept crying in my ears?") Clearly, Augustine's project of differentiating between "true pleasure" and false—or transient pleasures—directs his interpretation of the people who were near him.

Augustine's narration of his sexual experience provides another example of his unwillingness to recall any pleasure that was not the "true" pleasure of knowing and loving God. Despite his sexual maturity, a marriage was postponed, as both parents thought it would handicap his "hopes for the future":

> In these hopes both of my parents indulged too much—my father because he hardly thought of you at all and only thought in the most trivial way about me; my mother, because, in her view, these usual courses of learning would be, not only no hindrance, but an actual help to me in attaining you. (II.3)

And so, he continues, "I became evil for nothing"—that is, for no real pleasure.

The reader is led to expect that a juicy story will follow the slow build-up of the preceeding paragraphs. In these paragraphs, the different attitudes of Augustine's mother and his father, and his mother's warnings against fornication and especially adultery with "another man's wife" constitute a textual "tease" which is abruptly disappointed. Augustine frustrates the reader's prurient interest in his youthful sexual exploits by saying merely that he was "allowed to dissipate myself in all kinds of ways." He proceeds immediately to relate in detail an incident in which he and some companions stole pears they neither wanted nor enjoyed from a neighbor's tree. Augustine analyzes this deed minutely as an instance of gratuitous evil-doing. In his text, it takes the place of any concrete description of his sexual activity. Having identified the structure of all concupiscence as pleasureless "enjoyment" of compulsively acquired objects, Augustine uses the incident of the pear theft to illustrate rather than a more titillating story of sexual misbehavior.

Twentieth-century readers frequently express scorn for the "pear tree incident," calling it a trivial and uninteresting example of evil, nothing more than a demonstration of Augustine's neurotic verbal self-flagellation. Their irritation is, I think, at least partly to be explained by the fact that their hope for a good story about sex has been cultivated and disappointed. Augustine has engaged erotic interest, thereby strengthening the reader's attachment to the text, but failed to deliver what the text seems to promise. He will repeatedly use this textual strategy in order to produce in his reader the fascinated sexual interest, the increment of erotic energy that attaches her strongly to his *Confessions*. Each time he evokes the "torrent of pitch which boils and swells with the high tides of foul lust" (II.2), it is quickly followed by philosophical or theological reflection, or by the story of another kind of experience, rather than by a description of sexual activity. Why does Augustine repeatedly stimulate, only to frustrate, the reader's erotic interest?

Augustine is fully aware of the power of the written word for stimulating a reader to imitation of the narrated deeds. He has already noted his own "delight" in the "disgraceful" Homeric tales, citing the character in one of Terence's plays who regarded "Jupiter as an example to himself of how to seduce people" (I.16). Later in the *Confessions* Augustine's own susceptibility to imitate behavior he reads about will be further documented. On the basis of his own experience of being stimulated by reading, Augustine refuses to provide this potential temptation to his readers.

Moreover, generations of readers of the *Confessions* have found it difficult to believe the joyless picture Augustine paints of his sexual experience. Placed alongside vivid accounts of other aspects of his life, the narration of his life with the unnamed woman who lived with him in faithfulness for thirteen years and bore his son is remarkably bland:

> In those years I lived with a woman who was not bound to me in lawful marriage; she was one who had come my way because of my wandering desires and my lack of considered judgment; nevertheless I had only this one woman and I was faithful to her. And with her I learned by my own experience how great a difference there is between the self-restraint of the marriage covenant which is entered into for the sake of having children, and the mere pact made between two people whose love is lustful and who do not want to have children—even though, if children are born, they compel us to love them. (IV.2; also VIII.1)

It is difficult to reconcile this acknowledgment of sexual passion with the dispassionate prose with which Augustine recalls it. And this is the woman who, as Augustine said, was "torn from his side" when she returned to North Africa, the victim of his pursuit of a more advantageous marriage.

> My heart, which clung to her, was broken and wounded, and dripping blood. . . . Nor was the wound

healed [by Augustine's taking another mistress since the woman to whom he was engaged was still too young for marriage]. . . . It burned, it hurt intensely, and then it festered, and if the pain became duller, it became more desperate. (VI.15)

There are three possible explanations for the disparity between Augustine's acknowledgment of passion and the cool prose with which he described the relationship; two of them have already been suggested. First, Bishop Augustine would rather remember the pain than the pleasure in order to minimize his own—and the reader's—memory of "false" pleasures; secondly, he does not want to stir the reader to seek similar sexual relationships. But another reason is probably the one that was in the forefront of Augustine's mind while he wrote the *Confessions*. Augustine rationalizes presenting sex as more trouble than it's worth by insisting on his own compulsive attachment to it. Pursuit of sex, he consistently writes, was a "slavery" that *by definition* could not give pleasure because "a slave can't enjoy that to which he is enslaved." Augustine details the progress of enslavement:

From a perverse will came lust, and slavery to lust became a habit, and the habit, being constantly yielded to, became a necessity. These were like links, hanging each to each (which is why I call it a chain), and they held me fast in a hard slavery. (VIII.5)

Interwoven with his metaphor of the chained slave, Augustine uses images of food and nourishment to express the ungratifying nature of compulsive sexual activity. He describes himself as brought by concupiscence to a state of severe malnutrition. The objects of sex, power, and possession did not provide nourishment, even when he attained them. These objects are, Augustine insisted, good in themselves, but they are nevertheless consistently unsatisfying to the person who pursues them compulsively. A cumulative and increasingly serious lack of real nourishment is the only result of this pursuit: "For those who find their gratification in external things easily become empty and pour themselves out on things seen and temporal and, with starving minds, lick shadows" (IX.4). The pseudo nourishment of the habit of concupiscence is nothing but the gratification of a repetition compulsion. Suffering from starvation, the soul sinks into a state in which lethargy and anxiety are combined, a state in which the lethargy of a sleepwalker is assimilated to frenzied activity (IX.13). The quality of relationships with other human beings in this mode of operation is dramatically presented in Augustine's image of "eating one another up, as people do with their food" (IX.2). The behavior of the infant at the mother's breast is disguised, but structurally unaltered, in adult relationships.

Augustine's passionate pursuit of sexual pleasure was equalled by his passion for knowledge. Knowledge, for Augustine the young rhetor, constituted both pleasure and power. It was the promise of esoteric knowledge that drew him to the Manichees, reputedly learned men who had arrived in North Africa impressively carrying huge volumes they claimed to under-

stand and expound. As a young man, Augustine
retained his unlettered parents' exaggerated respect
for learning. He became a Manichaean "hearer" or dis-
ciple, and remained so for nine years. Soon, however,
he noticed some puzzling discrepancies between philosophical reasoning and what he came to call "the inter-
minable fables of the Manichees." His Manichaean
friends urged him to wait for the arrival of a learned
Manichaean named Faustus who was gifted with
"smoothness of language," and could explain these apparent inconsistencies in a satisfying way. Eventually
Faustus arrived, but he failed to convince the skeptical
Augustine, asking him to *believe* Mani's doctrines
rather than to examine them. In questioning Faustus
Augustine found that he was not educated in any of
the liberal sciences except literature; Faustus relied
heavily on rhetorical eloquence to mask his lack of real
knowledge. Disillusioned, Augustine "began to prefer
the Catholic faith" (VI.5), but he was still far from ready
to profess it.

Yet knowledge in itself was not enough. Augustine
was intellectually convinced of the truth of Catholic
faith by a series of reading experiences that began with
Cicero's *Hortensius* (III.4) at the age of nineteen and
continued with "some books written by the Platonists"
(VII.9). These books settled several intellectual problems, such as the problem of evil, for Augustine. Yet
they left him unsatisfied; he missed in them any suggestion that "The Word was made flesh and dwelt
among us." Intellectual assent to Catholic Christianity
was not Augustine's problem.

Augustine was particularly interested in the reality
of Christ's flesh because his own had thus far eluded

his efforts of control. He had long recognized the significance of his driven sexuality, namely that it was
sexual passion that captured and wounded his will,
causing a split between intellectual assent and desire.
He had begged God, "Make me chaste and continent,
but not yet" (VIII.7). "The truth is certain," Augustine
admonished himself, "but you are still weighed down
by your burden."

> My soul hung back; it refused to follow, and it could
> give no excuse for its refusal. All the arguments had
> been used already and had been shown to be false.
> There remained a mute shrinking; for it feared like
> death to be restrained from the flux of a habit by which
> it was melting away into death. (VIII.7)

Intellectual persuasion was not equivalent to existential conviction. His analysis of the abyss to be
crossed between intellectual understanding and the
energy necessary for creating a satisfying synthesis of
knowledge and conviction, from inertia to activity,
rests on precise observation:

> Now I could see it perfectly clearly. But I was still tied
> down. . . . The pack of this world was a kind of pleasant
> weight upon me, as happens in sleep, and the thoughts
> in which I meditated on you were like the efforts of
> someone who tries to get up but is so overcome with
> drowsiness that he sinks back again into sleep . . . we
> feel a sort of lethargy in our limbs . . . we put off the
> moment of shaking off sleep. . . . In just the same way
> I was quite certain that it was better to give myself up
> to your charity rather than to give in to my own desires;
> but, though the former course was a conviction to
> which I gave my assent, the latter was a pleasure
> to which I gave my consent. (VIII.5)

Augustine's inertia was, he noted, combined with a frenzied anxiety; though he longed for rest, this restlessness prevented him from yielding to the lassitude he felt. Two wills struggled for dominance within him, an old will, thoroughly woven into the body by habit, and a new will, which was "not yet strong enough to overpower the old will which by its oldness had grown hard in me." Augustine is a burden to himself; he is "on my own back" (VIII.7). He needs simultaneously to "relax a little from myself" (VII.14), and to be awakened, stimulated: "Come, Lord, act upon us and rouse us up and call us back! Fire us, clutch us, charm us with your sweet fragrance. Let us love, let us run!" (VIII.4)

The pleasure experiment has come to a dead end. A joyless Augustine "panted for honors, for money, for marriage," but recalls finding nothing but "bitterness and difficulty in following these desires" (VI.6). Occupied full-time in a single-minded pursuit of happiness, he has found the opposite. It is easy to forget— does Augustine want his readers to forget?—that at the time about which he wrote these words, he was at the peak of a successful career as a teacher of rhetoric, living in faithfulness to his partner of thirteen years, with a son he is proud of, and surrounded by dear and devoted friends he has known since childhood. Yet Augustine confesses himself to be "eaten up with anxieties," a "slave of lust," hating "the whole wearisome business of human life" (VI.14), in short, in a "drowned and sightless state" (VI.16).

In this state, Augustine came—was led, he writes, in retrospect—to the end of an agenda that had directed his values and his behavior from the infant's first gasp/grasping of breath, through the schoolboy's theft and the young man's relentless pursuit of sex and professional success.

The pressure is too great; something must give. Augustine, in a private garden with his friend from childhood, Alypius, enters fully into the conflict, worn out and used up by trying to keep it at bay: "I was mad and dying; but there was sanity in my madness, life in my death." His narration focuses on the physical effects of his internal struggle:

> In the middle of this storm of mental conflict I made many movements with my body—the kind of movements which people sometimes want to make, but cannot make, either because they have not the limbs, or because their limbs are bound or weakened by illness or in some way or other prevented from action. . . . I tore my hair, beat my forehead, locked my fingers together, clasped my knee. . .
>
> I was sick and in torture. . . . I turned and twisted in my chain. . . .
>
> A huge storm rose up within me, bringing with it a huge downpour of tears. . . . I flung myself on the ground and gave free rein to my tears. (VIII.8–12)

In the process of a second birth, Augustine reverts to the body language of the infant, to the inarticulate, desperate emotion of the newborn that can only be expressed in bodily motion.

Augustine's conversion was, as he had known it would need to be, a release from the compulsive pursuit of sex. In telling the story of his violent struggle, Augustine is on the verge of dangerous memories: he pictures his mistresses plucking at his sleeve, "mur-

muring softly" in his ear: "Are you getting rid of us?"
and "From this moment will you never for all eternity
be allowed to do this or that again?" Bishop Augustine
recoils from the memory:

> My God, what was it, what was it that they suggested
> in those words "this" or "that" that I have just written?
> I pray you in your mercy to keep such things from the
> soul of your servant. How filthy, how shameful were
> these things they were suggesting! (VIII.11)

But the voices grew fainter, the middle-aged Augustine
relates, as the young Augustine was strengthened in
his resolve. Continence, personified as a woman with
"chaste dignity, calm and serene, cheerful without
wantonness," approaches him to replace those other
women. She assures him both that many others have
succeeded in living chastely, and that he will not need
to accomplish this by his own power. The image of an
infant learning to walk is evoked in the advice Continence gives: "Why do you try to stand by yourself? . . .
Let him support you. Do not be afraid. He will not draw
away and let you fall. Put yourself fearlessly in his
hands" (VIII.11).

Still weeping uncontrollably, Augustine hears a
childish voice: "Take, read; take, read," it chants. Augustine immediately accepts the command as directed
to him; his first response is physical: "at once my face
changed." He goes to the place he has dropped the
"book of the Apostle":

> I snatched up the book, opened it, and read in silence
> the passage on which my eye first fell: "Not in rioting
> and drunkenness, not in chambering and wantonness,
> not in strife and envying: but put ye on the Lord Jesus

Christ and make not provision for the flesh in concupiscence."

The reading is transformative; no sooner had Augustine read these words than "it was as though my heart was filled with a light of confidence and all the shadows of my doubt were swept away" (VIII.12). In the telling, Augustine turns from the present tense in which he had narrated the conversion to the past tense to report Monica's joy on being informed of the event. Just as Augustine's hope has changed from being directed toward a wife and other worldly hopes, Monica's changes from the expectation of grandchildren to come from Augustine's flesh to the spiritual fruit of his conversion.

A direct exchange has been made in the process of Augustine's conversion: the "toys" or, literally, "sweet nothings" Augustine had treasured were dismissed—effortlessly, on Augustine's part—by the "true and supreme sweetness": "You cast them out, and you entered in to me to take their place" (IX.1). Augustine, who had feared that he would be "desperately unhappy" if he were deprived of a woman's embraces (VI.12), now embraces a happiness that is "sweeter than all pleasure" (IX.1). He has achieved the goal of his long search for the greatest pleasure.

Pleasure, it must be acknowledged, is one of the most notoriously indeterminate and variable of human experiences. Why, in the midst of professional achievement, friendships, and sexual relationships, did Augustine describe himself as pleasureless? What did Augustine *recognize* as pleasurable?

Two prominent features of his notion of pleasure are permanence and intensity. Defining pleasure in this way, however, creates a problem. Either permanence or intensity in isolation from the other would perhaps be achievable. One can take immense pleasure in elegant ideas, in beautiful and unchanging principles of mathematics, or even in a changeless God. But surely such abstractions fail to produce the intense delight of a single spring morning. And it is difficult, on the basis of sensory experience, to imagine pleasure that is both intense and permanent. The senses fatigue; they cannot sustain a receptive sensitivity to any stimulus for very long. But what Augustine wants is sensual experience that remains—or is continuously renewed at optimal excitment.

Augustine is a demanding lover of pleasure, and he claims, in fact, to have found an object that stimulates like this, that produces a quasi physical synesthesia that floods the body's senses as it does the "eye of the mind" (VII.1) and the "ear of the heart" (IV.5):

What do I love when I love you? Not the beauty of the body nor the glory of time, not the brightness of light shining so friendly to the eye, not the sweet and various melodies of singing, not the fragrance of flowers and ointments and spices, not manna and honey, not limbs welcome to the embraces of the flesh; it is not these that I love when I love my God. And yet I do love a kind of light, melody, fragrance, food, embracement when I love my God; for he is the light, the melody, the fragrance, the food, the embracement of my inner self— there where is a brilliance that space cannot contain, a sound that time cannot carry away, a perfume that no breeze disperses, a taste undiminished by eating, a clinging together that no satiety will sunder. (X.6)

Augustine's model of pleasure is one in which rest, peace, and equilibrium is held together with emotional intensity and permanence. The key to pleasure, for Augustine, was ideally not the sacrifice of some pleasures so that others could be cultivated. It was the ordering of all the pleasures of a human life so that those associated with enjoyment of objects in the sensible world would not usurp all of a person's attention and affection. When pleasures are constellated around a single object of love, he said, they can be enjoyed without fear of distraction. All the pleasurable beauty of the world can then be recognized as evidence of the consummate goodness of its creator.

The reason for orienting oneself to God, Augustine says, is that only here—at this psychic "place"—is ultimate pleasure possible. Although Augustine considers a single stable fulcrum as essential to human happiness, he is eager to "have it all." Multiplicity and variety exist—and are valuable—because the senses of mortal human bodies fatigue easily and must be restimulated continuously if they are to *perceive* the created world as good in each part, and as a whole, very good. Organized, collected multiplicity is order. Order guarantees that diversity and multiplicity will no longer be experienced as distraction and confusion. Like Aristotle's "golden mean," Augustine's idea of order holds in dynamic tension the full range of experience without diluting or bleaching its strength and colorfulness. Yet order can also be said to move in the direction of rest, in the sense—not of slackness or even relaxation,—but of equilibrium and stability: peace. An effective ordering must maintain life's intrinsic pleasure by providing the appropriate place for each of its variations. Pleasure, then, is not simple, but complex; the *Confessions* both documents and reproduces this complex pleasure.

This is Augustine's theory; it is somewhat at odds with his practice. Augustine felt himself to be what twentieth-century people might call a "sex addict," and there are pleasures that addicts must deny themselves in order to maintain equilibrium in their lives. For Augustine, sex was consuming, totalitarian. As an addict, it was not possible for him to enjoy a sexual relationship in freedom. And so his conversion revolved around the resolution of this problem area in his life. He sacrificed sexual activity in order to achieve the two "goods" he could not manage while he was sexually active—choice and control. He did not, it should be noted, in the *Confessions* or in his other works, press his own resolution on anyone else or describe celibacy as the norm for Christians who were serious about their faith. Nevertheless, his mastery of language ensured that his description of his own resolution was powerfully affecting, contributing to the subsequent glorification of the sexless life in Catholic Christianity.

In the next chapter, we turn from considering Augustine's painstaking description of an initially unrewarding but eventually satisfied search for the greatest possible sustained pleasure to examining some textual devices by which the *Confessions* itself produces a complex pleasure in its readers. We will ask: How was this "text of pleasure" constructed?

2

Textual Pleasure: "Where Can I Find the Books?"[11]

The text of pleasure is not necessarily the text that recounts pleasures.[12]

What if knowledge itself were delicious?[13]

How can we imagine what our lives should be without the illumination of other lives?[14]

Throughout the narrative of another person's life experience, especially when it is told as dramatically as Augustine's, holds perennial and intrinsic interest and pleasure for readers or hearers. Narrative alone would make the *Confessions* a text of pleasure. In this chapter, however, I will consider a further dimension of the pleasure of the text, namely, Augustine's use of several strategies that enhance readers' vigorous engagement with the text. The *Confessions* represents one side of an energetic conversation in which the reader's response is solicited and provoked. The pleasure that results from this conversation is not merely the simple pleasure of hearing a good story, but the complex pleasure of strong feelings—sometimes violent disagreement, sometimes frustration, sometimes "the—not inconsiderable—pleasure of resistance,"[15] and sometimes near-ecstatic recognition of the great beauty, "beauty so old and so new" (X.27), to which Augustine points through the beauty of his prose.

The primary training for any author is reading. From Augustine's own reading experience, he assumed that he knew what any reader expects to experience. And he expected the reader of the *Confessions* to be as affected as he was when he read. We must ask first, then: What was Augustine's reading practice? What did he expect his reader to experience? The simple answer to this latter question is that Augustine expected reading to be a powerful, life-changing experience. He gives several accounts of life-altering and -orienting experiences—his own and others—which revealed to him the potentially powerful effects of reading. His repeated use of the metaphor of fire in connection with reading expresses this. For example, Augustine described his own reading, at the age of nineteen, of Cicero's *Hortensius*. He credits his reading of this now lost work by a pagan author with dramatic results:

> It was this book which altered my way of feeling, turned my prayers to you, Lord, yourself, and gave me different ambitions and desires . . . What moved me was not the style but the matter. I was on fire, then, my God, I was on fire to leave earthly things behind and fly back to you. (III.4)

Augustine missed only one thing in the *Hortensius*: the "deeply treasured" name of Christ, imbibed with his mother's milk. He therefore decided to study the scriptures, but his first perusal was deeply disappointing. The Christian scriptures "seemed to me unworthy of comparison with the grand style of Cicero" (III.5). Later, after God has "rescued my tongue as you rescued my heart" (IX. 4), Augustine will revise his judgment of the scriptures, finding in his own earlier disappointment the evidence of his alienation from God. He will come to criticize, not the scriptures, but his own reading of them.

In spite of his early dissatisfaction with scripture, Augustine's own most intense and transformative reading experiences as a convert were his reading of scripture and devotional literature. In the *Confessions*, he combines the language and style of each, recounting his own journey to God by the use of scriptural phrases, interwoven through his narration. Because Augustine expected his confessions to act powerfully in the lives of his readers, he used in them the most powerful language he knew, a vocabulary of scriptural

phrases well known and richly evocative to his anticipated audience of fellow Christians. His memory of
hearing the story of Simplicianus's conversion may
have been in his mind as he crafted his own conversion
story. Hearing Simplicianus's conversion account, Augustine was "on fire to be like him" (VIII.5).

Shortly before Augustine's conversion, he heard
about another powerful reading experience. Ponticianus, finding Augustine reading the writings of Saint
Paul, told him about *his* own conversion, which was
precipitated by reading a life of Saint Antony (VIII.6).
Augustine describes Ponticianus's reading as a process of direct conversation with the text in which Ponticianus allowed the text to evaluate and judge his life
and to point the way to a new life. The metaphor of
birth expresses both the labor and the ultimate joy of
the experience:

> . . . he turned back to the book, troubled and perplexed
> by the new life to which he was giving birth. So he read
> on, and his heart, where you saw it, was changed, and,
> as soon appeared, his mind shook off the burden of the
> world. While he was reading and the waves in his heart
> rose and fell, there were times when he cried out
> against himself, and then he distinguished the better
> course and chose it for himself. (VIII.6)

For Augustine and his friends, reading was anything but a passive process. Augustine expected a powerful text to grasp him forcefully, but he also expected
to be active in the process, questioning both his own
life in the text's light and the text's truth in light of his
own experience.

Augustine's conversion was itself intimately intertwined with hearing and reading. The phrase that he heard at the moment of his conversion was *tolle, lege*; *tolle, lege* ("take, read"). To read, for Augustine, was to swallow, to assimilate, to digest, to incorporate, *to eat* the text. Is it accidental that the words *take, read* parallel the central words of the mass, familiar to Augustine from his boyhood: "take, eat" (*accipe, comedite*)? Receiving the overheard words *tolle, lege* as God's instruction directly to him, Augustine trusts and obeys. But even in his receptivity, he was not passive. Even in his condition of physical and mental stress, he considers and consciously interprets the words before he appropriates them:

> I began to think carefully of whether the singing of words like these came into any kind of game which children play, and I could not remember that I had ever heard anything like it before. (VIII.12)

He also identifies a precedent for his reading of the text:

> [I was] quite certain that I must interpret this as a divine command to me to open the book and read the first passage which I should come upon. For I had heard this about Antony: he had happened to come in when the Gospel was being read, and *as though the words read were spoken directly to himself*, had received the admonition: "Go, sell all that thou hast, and give to the poor, and thou shalt have treasure in heaven, and come and follow me." (VIII.12)

Retracing his steps, he snatched up the "book of the Apostle" he had been reading before he was overcome by emotion, "opened it, and read in silence the passage upon which my eyes first fell." The words Augustine reads are: "Not in rioting and drunkenness, not in chambering and wantonness, not in strife and envying: but put ye on the Lord Jesus Christ, and make not provision for the flesh in concupiscence" (VIII.12). These words—written and read—were strong catalysts, consolidating the gradual intellectual and emotional processes that warred in Augustine. In order to understand the transformative power of reading for him, it is necessary to take into account his excitement over a newly learned reading practice.

One of the most important experiences of Augustine's early days in Milan was the discovery of a new method of reading, one with which he had been unfamiliar in North Africa. He had been taught to read in a way that maximally engaged the body and senses: reading aloud, seeing and hearing words, simultaneously moving the lips, an art of tone and emphasis, expressive reading. So he was astonished as a young man, new to the sophisticated imperial capital of Milan, to witness Ambrose reading silently: "When he was reading his eyes went over the pages and his heart looked into the sense, but voice and tongue were resting" (VI.3). Together with his mother, Augustine sat in silence "for a long time" watching him, speculating on why he chose to read in this strange fashion. This silent reading practice, reading without the body, fascinated him.

Moreover, in Augustine's time, reading aloud was a public practice, usually conducted in a company of people, so that illiterate people could benefit from hearing words that they could not read. Ambrose read both in silence and in private, observed but not heard, his thoughts about what he was reading unspoken, inaccessible to others.

Augustine immediately began to practice silent, private reading. In *Confessions* IX.4, he reconstructs his first passionate reading of the Psalms of David as a newly converted catechumen. He read, he says, with intense excitement and a neurasthenic responsiveness: [16]

> My God, how I poured out my heart to you. . . . How I cried aloud to you in these Psalms! How they fired me toward you! How I burned to utter them aloud. . . . I trembled with fear, and then again I was on fire with hope and exultation . . . and all these emotions were shown in my eyes and in my voice . . . I listened and trembled . . . I cried out as I read this with my outward eye and inwardly recognized its truth . . . my heart cried out from its depths. . . . As I read, my heart became on fire . . . my heart boiled. (IX.4)

At the time of his writing of the *Confessions*, about a decade after the cataclysmic event that was to alter the course of the rest of his long and productive life, Augustine provided his readers with the potentially transformative narrative of his conversion. Reading without the body, silent, private reading, was precisely the sort of reading practice that Augustine imagined for readers of the *Confessions*. There is no indication anywhere in the *Confessions* that Augustine expected groups of people to read it aloud together. On the contrary, it always addresses the individual, alone with his private thoughts and memories. Twentieth-century readers, deeply familiar with a private reading practice that developed in the Christian West from devotional reading, need to remind ourselves of the oddity of private reading in Augustine's time. In writing the *Confessions*, Augustine adopted and adapted an esoteric reading practice and unknowingly provided it with one of the texts that would perpetuate this practice and give it its greatest popularity.

For *whom* was—or is—the *Confessions* a pleasurable text? In his *Retractationes*, written in the year before his death, Augustine reviewed his corpus of writings, commenting on and correcting each of them. He says explicitly that in the *Confessions* he intended, and feels that he has achieved, both his own pleasure as author and the reader's pleasure. It is always an encouraging indication of a book's potential to pleasure the reader when its author testifies, as Augustine does, that the book was enjoyable to write. Augustine's *Confessions* stimulated him to happy praise, he says, when they were written, and "they work this in me when they are read."[17] Yet the *Confessions* was not an easy book to write; we should not confuse pleasure with ease. He also frequently exclaimed about its difficulty:

> For me, Lord, certainly this is hard labor, hard labor inside myself, and I have become to myself a piece of difficult ground, not to be worked over without much sweat. (X.16)

Although he acknowledged the difficulty of his project of remembering and revealing himself in language, there is, in addition to his testimony in the *Retractationes*, additional evidence that Augustine took pleasure in writing and rereading the *Confes-*

sions. Throughout the text many abrupt interjections both explicitly acknowledge and signal a moment of particular pleasure. Sometimes he frankly states: "It is a pleasure to me, Lord, to confess to you" (IX.4). At other times, spontaneous ejaculations interrupt narrative accounts as well as densely argued philosophical or theological points when Augustine is temporarily overwhelmed by the pleasure he feels in recalling his experiences and thoughts: "Come, Lord, excite us and call us back! Inflame and ravish and charm us with your sweetness! Let us love! Let us run!" (VIII.4)

Augustine was apparently not alone in his pleasure in writing and reading the *Confessions*: "they have given much pleasure, and do give pleasure, to many brethren I know." He asks rhetorically in *De dono perseverantiae* 20.53: "Which of my smaller works could be more widely known or give greater pleasure than my *Confessions*?" Augustine was gratified to hear of his project's success. While he was a rhetor, he received applause for speeches containing "a lot of lies," even though his audience recognized the lies (VI.6). Words, although they are potentially "choice and valuable vessels," if they do not carry veracity and profundity, are "mere smoke and wind" (I.17). Clearly, some of Augustine's professional pride as a rhetor in *pleasing* by the skillful use of language has carried over to his authorship as a Christian bishop.

Augustine seemed not to notice the similarity of his Christian occupation to that of his preconversion profession. Characteristically, he exaggerated their differences in order to emphasize the complete change in his life brought about by conversion. Shortly after his conversion, a physical aversion to the profession of teaching rhetoric prompted Augustine's decision to leave it; the body, again, as in the account of his conversion is both site and symbol of "movements of the soul":

> My lungs had begun to give way as the result of overwork in teaching. I found it difficult to breathe deeply; pains in the chest were evidence of the injury and made it impossible for me to speak loudly or for long at a time . . . I was being almost forced and compelled to give up this burden of teaching. (IX.2)

Augustine acknowledges the psychosomatic nature of these symptoms:

> What had helped me in the past to bear my hard labor had been the desire to make money. The desire was now gone . . . I began actually to be pleased that in this illness I had an excuse. (IX.2)

Augustine the bishop remarked in recalling his resignation: "You rescued my tongue as you rescued my heart. . . . My writing was now done in your service" (IX.4). Yet, now that, in the *Confessions*, Augustine speaks truth, the skill that made him a successful rhetor has not vanished. He hopes that readers will not be conscious of his skill and artfulness, even though it is evident in every sentence. We turn now to a closer examination of some of the major devices that serve to keep readers in strong engagement with the *Confessions*, the primary requirement for a pleasurable "read."

Two of these strategies will occupy us in the rest of this chapter: indeterminacy of address and unresolved contradiction. Both of these features render the first eight books of the *Confessions* volatile, incomplete, unstable—and thus call for readers' co-authorship. In Chapter 3, we will consider the *Confessions* as an erotic text, certainly a feature that heightens reader engagement. In these two chapters our attention will continue to be primarily on the first nine books of the *Confessions*. Theological and philosophical speculations dominate Books 10 to 13, and rather different concerns and strategies mark these books; I will focus on them in the final chapter.

The *Confessions* is addressed to multiple hearers/readers. As the text continuously slides from one addressee to another, the reader's pleasure in feeling directly addressed shifts to the rather different pleasure of overhearing a communication addressed to someone else. Along with the frequent interjections and ejaculations that interrupt the text, indeterminacy of address also opens the text, keeping it mobile, circulating, accessible but not possessable.

Augustine holds in suspension several different audiences: God, "people," and himself—self-talk. The ostensible addressee of the *Confessions* is God—"you have made us for yourself, and our hearts are restless until they rest in you" (I.1). Yet, in the next paragraph, Augustine asks (whom?), "How shall I pray to my God?" Clearly, he does not imagine his conversation with God to be taking place in a closet, as Jesus taught his disciples to pray, far from the eyes and ears of other human beings. At times he specifies his ideal readers;

at other times, he simply addresses them: "fellow citi-
zens, fellow pilgrims: those who have gone before and
those who follow after and those who are on the road
with me" (X.4). As I have already mentioned, Augustine
was also especially eager to find readers who will not
laugh at him (IV.1). And the *Confessions* is self-talk, a
method of recollecting himself. Finally, the text's mobility and multiplicity of address invites—even compels—
the modern reader unanticipated by Augustine to
enter!

Moreover, Augustine was well aware of the persua-
sive effectiveness in positioning readers to "overhear"
his private confessions to his confessor, especially one
that promises titillating scatological detail. In his demonstration "reading" of several verses from the Psalms
of David discussed above (IX.4), Augustine explicitly
specifies that it would be important for those he wishes
to convert to Catholic Christianity to *overhear* his passionate exegesis, rather than think themselves directly
addressed:

I should have liked [the Manichees] to have been standing somewhere near me (without my knowing that they
were there) and to have seen my face and heard what I
said when in this time of quietness I read the fourth
Psalm, and to have seen what effect those words of the
Psalm had on me . . . I should have liked them to have
heard me without my knowing whether they heard.
Otherwise they might think that what I was saying
when I read those verses was being said because of
them. And in fact I should neither say the same things
nor speak in the same way, if I realized that they were
watching me and listening to me. And even if I did say
the same things, they would not have understood how

> I was speaking with myself and to myself in front of you, out of the natural feelings of my soul. (IX.4)

Both his own self-consciousness in knowing he was being listened to and his hearer's resistance to his rhetorical strategies would have weakened the force of the communication he imagines.

In the *Confessions*, Augustine has carefully crafted a communication structured in precisely this way. The speaker/author's back is to his audience; he pretends to ignore them and to speak without inhibition or restriction to God; yet sprinkled throughout are signals that, in fact, it is not God, who, after all, knows and sees all things, that needs to be made aware of Augustine's story. Rather it is the reader who must be persuaded, inspired to imitate, converted:

> Anyone who cares to can read what I have written and interpret it as he likes. (IX.12)

> This is what I want to do in my heart, in front of you, in my confession, and in my writing before many witnesses. (X.1)

> Why, then, do I bother to let human beings hear my confessions? . . . Human beings are very inquisitive about other people's lives, very lazy in improving their own. Why should they want to hear from me what I am when they do not want to hear from you what they are? (X.3)

Appearing to address God—addressing God—Augustine interjects references to his eavesdroppers. To ignore them completely would risk their loss of interest; Augustine must keep his readers listening by frequent subtle acknowledgments of their presence.

The first nine books of the *Confessions* stay close to the process of Augustine's life, to his progress toward conversion. Although they narrate that process, they also reproduce the strains, anxiety, and energy of the life they narrate. Augustine's writing style—full of interruptions, surprises, alternation between detailed description and failure to supply important information—reflects Augustine's life, reminding us that people do not necessarily think systematically and act consistently with what they have figured out. Issues surface at particular times because events and emotions draw them to the surface, present them for examination and work. They "come up" for attention. Most people can tolerate a rather high level of logical contradiction in their ideas, values, and actions. These contradictions can even coexist without friction; they simply respond to different intellectual, psychological, and social occasions and situations. Furthermore, in life logically contradictory ideas can complement, correct, or provide alternatives, one of which may work better in one situation than another.

When we struggle as scholars to exhibit the inner consistency of an author's thought, we satisfy ourselves, catering to our own assumptions and predilections. However, to the extent that we resolve and remove contradictions that our text holds "in suspension," we both distort the author's ideas and remove the tension, discomfort, and life-likeness of the text, making it bland. We bleach out its strident, sometimes confusing colors, and leave it orderly, consistent, boring. In short, we do what Augustine *instructs* his readers to do rather than what he himself *does* as an author. The explicit agenda of the *Confessions* is an ordering of experience and world so that ideas and desires do not contradict one another, but *fit*—and can be shown to fit—each in its proper place. What Augustine *does* in his text, however, is to maintain unresolved contradictions that disturb a reader, keeping her awake, irritated, engaged. Is not a "text of pleasure" *necessarily* a text containing contradictions that create tension, that provoke and stimulate author and reader to attempt to overcome them *as* contradictons in order to display them as mutually supporting and reinforcing insights?

Unresolved textual contradictions do not necessarily signal the author's confusion about the topic about which he writes. Rather, as I suggested above, contradictory explanatory theses deal with phenomena more adequately in one existential situation than in another. And the juxtaposition of pairs of contrasting entities— God and human, body and soul, flesh and spirit—does not necessarily reveal the presence of a dualistic metaphysic. Metaphysical dualism, which is found less often than generally supposed in Augustine's thought, entails not merely contrasted, but mutually exclusive entities. Augustine's contrasting pairs are mutually necessary in that each requires and defines its opposite. As contradictions, they generate a textual instability that creates discomfort, and therefore attention, in the reader.

The *Confessions* is riddled with contradictions that have, for sixteen hundred years, irritated and stimulated readers to excited labor and play. The simplest level of contradicton in the *Confessions* is the ubiquitous oxymorons Augustine uses, for example, "living death . . . dying life," "sane madness" (VIII.8);

Augustine uses these tightly packaged verbal contradictions to signal an occasion of great complexity and
intensity. He does not pause to break these oxymorons
down, to dilute them into discursive explanation, but
allows them to boggle the mind, to block the reader's
satisfaction along with her impression of intellectual
grasp.

But figures of speech—oxymorons—are only the
most obvious and least disturbing level of contradiction in the *Confessions*. There are also contradictions
even in Augustine's "resolutions." Although he claims
to have solved to his own satisfaction the urgent puzzles of his youth, contradictions remain. The major
contradicitons of the *Confessions* revolve around bodies, their status and their meaning. God's body, initially a problem for Augustine in that he cannot
imagine a body that is not extended in space, remains
contradictory in Augustine's attempts throughout the
Confessions to understand and explain God's existence and activity. Christ's body also puzzles Augustine; he struggled to understand "divinity in the
weakness that it had put on by wearing our 'coat of
skin'" (VII.18). Finally, the status and meaning of human bodies and the world's body with all its creatures
constantly occupy—and elude—Augustine's effort to
place bodies in a coherent and stable order. These lively
and volatile bodies consistently refuse to stay in the
places to which Augustine has assigned them; their
insubordination, however, creates a large part of the
pleasurable tension of the text. Let us look more carefully at each of these contradictions and their textual
effects.

God's body: Augustine's first difficulty in thinking

about God was his inability to think of God as anything but "a corporeal substance, extended in space" (VII.1).

> So I . . . considered that whatever was not extended in space, whether diffused or condensed, or swelling out or having some such qualities or being capable of having them, must be, in the full sense of the word, nothing. The images in my mind were like the shapes I was used to seeing with my eyes. . . . I thought of you as an immensity through infinite space, interfused everywhere throughout the whole mass of the universe and extending beyond it in every direction for distances without end, so that the earth should have you, the sky should have you, all things should have you, and they should be bounded in you, but you should be boundless. (VII.1)

Augustine's image of an infinitely extended God, filling all things, however, was problematic in that it posited a God susceptible to corruption. Augustine found a changeable God intolerable on psychological as well as logical grounds. Even as he struggles to form an idea of God, there are certain commitments he will not negotiate: God exists; God is unchangeable; God cares for human beings; and God will judge them. These beliefs were "firmly and irrevocably rooted in my mind" (VII.7). And the image of a God whose body fills all things fails both to specify how God can be unchangeable and to show how and why that God can be a personal God who cares for people. Augustine's two notions about God are in conflict: each identifies a different arena and method for searching for God. Can God be found in the created world, in the beauty of God's creation? Or must one shut out created beauty in order to search for a God accessible only to the mind? Augustine continues to use both methods—inspection of sensory objects and introspection which begins by rejecting sensible things.

Augustine describes his search for God in the sensible world of bodies and objects: "And what is this God?" he asks the earth, all the things that are on the earth, the sea, creeping things with living souls, the blowing breezes and the cosmic air, heaven, the sun, moon, and stars:

> I said to all those things which stand about the gates to my senses: "Tell me about my God . . . tell me something about him." And they cried out in a loud voice: "He made us." My question was in my contemplation of them, and their answer was in their beauty. (X.6)

While using this inductive method, Augustine uses created things to focus his attention: the soul, he says, "rises out of its lethargy, supporting itself on created things" (V.1). Moreover, he does not subsequently pass over, or go beyond, sensible things in order to find God, but looks more deeply into them. And sensible things do not lie; they tell him plainly, we are not your God. Yet, as the creation of God, they can give important information about the kind of creator they have: "their answer was in their beauty," which witnesses to that of the Great Beauty which was their origin. Augustine asks rhetorically: "Is not this appearance of the universe evident to all whose senses are not deranged?" Furthermore, sensible objects do not mislead the inquirer by presenting a beautiful appearance; their structural beauty exceeds even that of their surface beauty.

Yet Augustine is not content with the information

he receives from sensible objects. There are two problems with their testimony: first, their surface beauty
can capture the unwary lover; second, perception of
sensible objects is not unique to the human race but
is also shared by animals. Augustine states the first
problem in this way: "By loving these things, [people]
become subject to them, and subjects cannot judge"
(X.6). If the objects of the sensible world are to reveal
God, a faculty of educated discernment must be
brought to perception. The passive viewer—one who
does not insist on "the question" ("What is this
God?")—will never receive the answer: "He made us."
Many people, as well as "animals, small and great, see
[the world], but cannot ask the question." And Augustine also finds it necessary to "pass on beyond" perception and its evidence, since "the horse and the mule
have it too" (X.7). He has used one epistemological
method, finding it fruitful, but not decisive in its information about God.

At the same time—just before the conversion of his
will in book 8—Augustine found an alternative explanation of God. In "some books written by the Platonists," Augustine found a transcendent God. Instructed
by these books to search for God as an "unchangeable
light" within his own soul, Augustine experienced this
God as he "by stages" shed his earlier images of God as
a body.

> And so I went by stages from the body to the soul which
> perceives by means of the bodily senses, and from this
> to the inner power of the soul to which the bodily
> senses present external things . . . from this point I
> went on to the faculty of reason to which sense data
> are referred for judgment. It then, as it were, raised

itself up to the level of its own understanding, freed my thoughts from the tyranny of habit, and withdrew from those crowds of contradictory phantasms. . . . And then, in the flash of a trembling glance [*trepidantus aspectus*], my mind arrived at that which is [*id quod est*]. . . . I had not the power to keep my eye steadily fixed; in my weakness I felt myself falling back and returning again to my habitual ways, carrying nothing with me except a loving memory of it and a longing for something which may be described as a kind of food of which I had perceived the fragrant aroma but which I was not yet able to eat. (VII.17)

This God is beyond images drawn from sensory experience, beyond human imagination which is inevitably informed by sensible objects, and beyond accessibility by means of the human repertoire of perception and logical thought. Augustine understood this God through an experience of being ravished[18] by God's beauty; almost immediately, however, he was torn away by the weight of the habits of physical existence. Augustine's problem of a method for experiencing and thinking of God is unresolved. He has identified two methods, each of which assumes quite different and contradictory roles for sensible objects: Is sensible beauty the starting point in a search for God so that the seeker must look more deeply *into* bodies in order to learn something about the God who created them? Or are all bodies and objects to be dismissed, excluded from a search for God that begins with the human mind but must necessarily transcend the mind's changeableness if it is to achieve even a "trembling glance" of "that which is?" Augustine does not decide between the two methods; both omit something of great importance to him. Together, however, in a contradiction that works more as cyclical oscillation than as impasse, Augustine finds them mutually corrective and thus necessary to sustain in suspension. This contradiction in Augustine's assessment of the role and status of human bodies in the search for God renders the text questionable, problematic, incomplete, *interesting.*

Christ's body: The issue of method was made even more gripping for Augustine by his struggle to understand Christ's divine and human natures. If Christ was really divine, his bodily existence on earth was initially, he tells his readers, impossible for him to understand. Indeed, it is only in coming to recognize Christ as indispensable *mediator* between God and human beings that Augustine began to *enjoy* God. The missing quality, that which had made him fall away from the vision of "that which is," was a humility he learned only by embracing "Jesus in his humility" and weakness as God.

> He built for himself a humble dwelling out of our clay, by means of which he might detach from themselves those who were to be subdued and bring them over to himself, healing the swelling of their pride and fostering their love, so that instead of going further in their own self-confidence they should put on weakness, seeing at their feet divinity in the weakness that it had put on by wearing our "coat of skin"; and then, weary, they should cast themselves down upon that divinity which, rising, would bear them up aloft. (VII.18)

But the meaning of the scriptural words, "I am the way, the truth and the life," was hard-won by Augustine: "This was not the way I thought then." He admired the virgin birth of Christ "as an example of how temporal things should be despised for the sake of gaining immortality," but did not have "the faintest notion of the mystery contained in 'The Word was made flesh'" (VII. 18).

Augustine describes his own inadequate understanding of the divinity and humanity of Christ as well as that of his friend, Alypius. On the one hand, he could not imagine that God could be born of the Virgin Mary, literally "sifted together" with her flesh, without defilement by that flesh (V. 10). Yet Augustine thought of Christ as fully human, a man "to be preferred to others, not because he was Truth in person, but because of the exceptional qualities of his human nature and his more perfect participation in wisdom" (VII. 19). He cannot see how divinity *and* humanity can coexist in one person without contamination of the divine by the human nature. Alypius, on the other hand, held what later came to be called "the error of the Apollinarian heretics" in imaging Jesus as a God clothed in flesh, but lacking a human soul (VII. 19). Yet it was not primarily misunderstandings that thwarted Augustine's search for God. Rather it was that he was "puffed up with my knowledge" and "the swelling of my pride; it was as though my cheeks had swollen up so that I could not see out of my eyes" (VII. 7). This self-important blindness, by young adulthood a habitual posture toward the world, held Augustine so that he was still "too weak to be able to enjoy" God: "if I had not sought the way to [God] in Christ our Saviour, what would have been finished would have been my soul" (VII. 20).

Fortunately, Augustine's driven search continued:

he continued to read. However, in addition to missing any reference to Christ Jesus in "those books of the Platonists," Augustine says, "humility was not a subject which those books would ever have taught me." And humility, as revealed in the human Jesus, was precisely the "strength" Augustine needed in order to enjoy God. He learned the difference between "those who see their goal without seeing how to get there and those who see the way which leads to that happy country which is there for us not only to perceive but to live in" (VII.20).

Now Augustine began to read Paul "very greedily," finding in the scriptures everything he had found true in the Platonist authors he had read—and more. In the scripture, "one is not only instructed so as to see you . . . but also so as to grow strong enough to lay hold on you" (VII.21). Without settling the question of how divinity and humanity could coexist,[19] Augustine is content to come to an understanding of Christ as mediator, the *method* or road to God. He understands Christ's human and divine nature as logical contradictions that are nevertheless *necessary*; in discovering humility, he has found the strength to hold them together and thus to identify the road to God. The way, he says, is "first humility, secondly humility, and thirdly humility." Now Augustine does not require conceptual smoothness in his ideas about God, but rather a concrete and energizing connection with God. It was the human Christ who made the difference between the presumption of the learned Platonist books and the humility that is required "to walk along the road by which he will arrive and see [God] and lay hold on [God]" (VII.20). The "face and look of pity" and the "tears of confession" are the method of access to God, not the pride of intellectual grasp.

Two further contradictions relating to bodies are present in the *Confessions*, and they should be mentioned here briefly, although I will discuss them more fully in chapter 3: human bodies and the world's body. We have seen that far from "disdaining the body," Augustine pays the minutest attention to physical movements, feelings, and appearances in order to identify the state of the soul. Emotions, yearnings, even the truth of a human life are described as somatic; the soul's movements are describable only as physical events. We have also seen in the earlier part of this chapter that living things and the earth's body provide important information about God to the intent questioner. Certainly, bodies have a high epistemological status in Augustine's search for God.

Yet Augustine also assumes—and reveals—a hierarchical ranking of human attributes and capacities in which the soul has far greater value than the body. Augustine switches, sometimes with remarkable rapidity, from privileging bodies as site and symbol of subjectivity to describing the soul as vastly superior to the lowly and problematic body. Augustine's formula is the following: the human soul is inferior to God, and the body is inferior to the soul; if the soul is in a state of insubordination to God, it loses its control over its own body; it is attracted by—and thus is connected to—every physical object that crosses its path in the anxious fear that something will be missed.[20] The created order is overturned by the disorderly, or concupiscent, affections:

I was superior to [things which are in space], but inferior to [God]. . . . This was the correct admixture—that
I should remain in your image and, by serving you, be
master of the body. . . . But when I arrogantly rose up
against you . . . these inferior things became above me
and kept me under, and there was no loosening of their
hold and no chance of breathing. (VII.7)

What is at stake is not the value of human bodies,
living beings, or the natural world, but the attitude
with which they are sought. The trouble with bodies
is that they are moribund, subject to corruption. Yet
their very corruptibility testifies to the goodness of
their creation and existence: if they were "to be deprived of all good, they will cease to exist altogether. . .
so long as they exist they are good." The problem of
evil, Augustine saw, was not to be settled by assigning
evil to bodies:

So I saw plainly and clearly that you have made all
things good, nor are there any substances at all which
you have not made. And because you did not make all
things equal, therefore they each and all have their existence; because they are good individually, and at the
same time they are altogether very good, because our
God made all things very good. (VII.12)

In spite of the fact that "all things are very good,"
they are, for Augustine, untrustworthy in two ways:
because they are finite, they cannot absorb and fulfil
infinite longing; and, we will see when we focus, in
chapter 4, on Augustine's resolution of his scattered
and driven longings, "things" remain problematic—
magic—for him in their capacity to distract him by

their surface beauty from recognition of their deep beauty as created beings. Augustine's contradictory account of the meaning and value of created things—at once good and dangerous—is not resolved in the *Confessions*.

Certainly the absence of contradiction where it can be achieved—that is, within carefully limited segments of logical reasoning—is among the finest achievements of human thought. Yet unresolved contradictions in a text create a pleasurable tension; they function to invite the reader into the text as conversation partner, opponent, supporter, and co-author. Attempting to remove textual contradictions by explaining their inner coherence and demonstrating their consistency, scholars often simultaneously remove much of the reader-author's pleasure. That is why commentary is usually so much less vivid, engaging, and interesting than the text it seeks to display. It is not the case that all authors intend and must achieve—or be helped by their interpreter to achieve—consistency of thought. This assumption excludes the possibility that by the skillful use of unresolved contraditions the author purposely constructed the reader's disequilibrium, and thus her focused attention.

Augustine was acutely aware of the role of dis-ease, disequilibrium, and tension in producing pleasure. He ponders this very topic meticulously, exhaustively, in book 8. He begins, "O good God, what is it in human beings that makes them rejoice more when a soul that has been despaired of and is in very great danger is saved than when there has always been hope and the danger has not been so serious?" He puzzles over the apparent perversity that requires a prior discomfort, distress, or anxiety to augment the pleasure that accompanies the alleviation of the tension. He multiplies examples; "the evidence is everywhere, simply crying out: 'it is so'" (VIII.3). He cites scriptural parables of the lost sheep, the lost coin, and the prodigal son. "What is it in the soul," he asks, "that makes it take more pleasure in the finding or recovery of things it loves than in the continual possession of them?" Victorious generals, storm-tossed sailors, the illness of a friend: all confirm Augustine's analysis of how "more pleasure" is achieved by a prior condition of lack.

In contrast to God, who is always the same, rejoicing in the spiritual and material creation, human beings require the cyclic oscillation of deprivation and satisfaction if they are to achieve the greatest pleasure. Even the ordinary pleasures of life are sought by purposely cultivating "difficulty and discomfort which are voluntary and self-chosen." Hunger and thirst create pleasure in eating and drinking; lengthy engagements produce a pleasure in sexual satisfaction that would not exist if marriage were quicker. Alternations "between deprivation and fulfillment, between discord and harmony" characterize not only "disgraceful" but also legitimate pleasures. "Everywhere we find that the more pain there is first, the more joy there is after" (VIII.4). Surely an author so sensitive to degrees of pleasure and to the amount of tension needed to produce each increment of pleasure, and who insists that his *Confessions* is a text of pleasure, consciously retained the contradictions that promote the pleasure of the text.

In this chapter I have considered Augustine's expectations for an effective book, a good read. Entertainment was not his goal in writing, as it was not his experience in reading. His own reading experiences, as well as those of his friends, led him to understand that reading—whether philosophical treatises like Cicero's *Hortensius*, or narratives of conversions, or scripture—could transform life. The truth can be found in books, but "where can I find the books?" Augustine anguished in his preconversion days (VI.11). Augustine hopes that the *Confessions* will be one of the books that points the way to truth. Yet in order to point effectively, not merely to intellectual truth but to truth that has the power to alter lives, his text must first create in the reader an intense, energetic, engrossing engagement. Although he rejected the profession of rhetoric, his considerable rhetorical skill—his "rescued tongue"—is not discarded, but "my writing was now done in your service."[21] It is now used to engage his reader in a dialogue in which the reader's life could be decisively altered.

3

The Erotic Text: "Scratching the Itching Scab"[22]

Eroticism is calm passion.[23]

That deep and irreplaceable knowledge of my capacity for joy comes to demand from all of my life that it be lived within the knowledge that such satisfaction is possible. [24]

As we began to see in chapter 1, Augustine shows remarkable skill in engaging readers' erotic curiosity only to refuse to satisfy it. His goal is to produce erotic interest and thus to supplement and intensify readers' multiple and complex attachments to the *Con-*

fessions; yet the text's eroticism must be firmly integrated and sublimated to the religious messages he
desires to communicate. We have also examined some
of the textual strategies by which the *Confessions* constructs its reader as voyeur in relation to an erotic text,
a text full of partial disclosures, vivid sensual metaphors, tantalizing gaps, and earnest appeals for the
reader's understanding and indulgence. In this chapter I will consider more directly Augustine's sexual experience and its role in his life and in his authorship.
Augustine's sexual experience is a topic at once titillating and frustrating, limited by his own self-expo-
sures and reticences, and—last but not least—
singularly vulnerable to distortions caused by the interpreter's personal and cultural assumptions about
sexuality.

I will attempt to offset distortions by exposing at
the outset the interpretive lens through which I read
Augustine's descriptions and interpretations of sex. In
general, my reading of Augustine's interpretation of
sex is informed by my society's acceptance of sex as
a positive, valuable, and pleasurable activity when it
occurs in relationships of mutuality and equality. Seen
through this lens, Augustine's sexual "lust" seems
"normal" and his failure to appreciate and enjoy it
seems overscrupulous and ungrateful.

However, as a late twentieth-century woman, I am
also keenly aware that sexual desire is socially constructed, that there is, as far as can be detected, no
unsocialized sexuality, no sexuality which is innocent
and individual until it is forced to serve society's eco-
nomic and reproductive needs. Sexualization is a central feature of the socialization of every individual.

Moreover, sexuality is gendered: women and men in all
known societies are expected and trained, in myriad
ways, to think, respond, and behave differently from
each other. Men's and women's roles in societies are
also different; their access to power is gendered, as well
as governed by class and race. In Western societies,
designed and administered by men, most men have
more power than most women, so that heterosexual
"relationships of mutuality and equality" seldom exist
between a man and a woman in anything but—at
best—an artificially secluded private sphere.

Both class and gendered power are evident in Augustine's relationships: his partner of thirteen years
came from a lower class than he did. Although he was
not from a wealthy family, Augustine was able to im-
prove his social standing by education and ability. Augustine, who had everything *but* wealth and nobility,
could rather easily add these by marrying "up." The
marriage he had contracted with an heiress cost him
nothing more than the sacrifice of the woman he had
lived with, an appreciable sacrifice as he described it,
but one he was prepared to make since it promised
wealth and a wider sphere of influence than he could
achieve on the basis of his skills alone. The end of this
relationship did not require him to return to his home
to live out his days in celibate devotion, even though—
interestingly—this is approximately what occurred.
Augustine had options—certainly he had job opportu-
nities—which were not accessible to his companion.
His upward mobility as a rhetor, we should notice, was
not subverted but enhanced by his conversion to Catholic Christianity; that he, as a bishop, could become so
rapidly the social equal of Ambrose, who was born into

wealth and nobility, was one of the effects of the emerging professionalism of Christian clergy in the late fourth century.

Sensitized both by my experience and by reading to the role of gendered sexualization in establishing and reinforcing unjust social arrangements, I can detect two reasons for Augustine's rejection of sexual activity. First, it is not difficult to understand why a sensitive and responsible person might choose not to participate in an arena of human life so burdened with conditioned responses, so culturally overdetermined, so, in Augustine's term, "unfree." Secondly, according to his own report, Augustine suffered from addiction to sex; he called it "slavery." There are good things that the addict cannot permit himself, though others who do not find them so difficult to control can enjoy them. Augustine wrote a speculative treatise on "The Good of Marriage"; he was able to appreciate it, even to recommend it in the abstract, but he despaired of his own ability to live an integrated sexuality. As a late twentieth-century North American, living in a society in which addictions of many kinds have reached epidemic levels, I can respect Augustine's sacrifice of sexual activity in exchange for an integrated life, a life in which his commitments were chosen and realistically consonant with his capacity to remain faithful to them.

Finally, I am a woman, reading about a man's sexual experience. I am judgmental of Augustine's authorial treatment of all the women who appear in his text. None of them stands in her own light, the subject of her own experience; all are evaluated according to their role in Augustine's heroic epic. This was, perhaps, painfully predictable. However, the strange discovery I have made in rereading the *Confessions* is that, in my former readings, I had obediently assumed the position of the sympathetic male colleague for whom Augustine wrote. The *Confessions* was not written to be read by a woman; to read it with "understanding" was to read it as a man—an educated skill; as the song says, "it's second nature to me now/like breathing out and breathing in." The difficult and interesting task, then, was to deliberately engage my gendered experience in reading,[25] to notice what I would not notice if I continued to read as the sympathetic male colleague for whom Augustine wrote. From this perspective, I noticed not only Augustine's actual and textual treatment of women, but also that the metaphor that dominates his construction of pleasure is male sexuality. I suspect that in spite of his loud and frequent disclaimers, Augustine learned more than he acknowledged from sex, that he learned "the deep and irreplaceable knowledge of [his] capacity for joy" from his sexual experience, and that it was precisely *this* experiential knowledge from which Augustine extrapolated his model of spiritual pleasure. I will endeavor to substantiate this suspicion a bit later.

Two further aspects of this chapter need brief explanation: first, why I have chosen to discuss Augustine's women in a context in which they can only appear as objects of, or in the case of his mother, protesters against Augustine's polymorphous lust. Surely I should not replicate the assumed male world of a long literary tradition which places anything to be said about women under the topic of sex. The tacit basis for this commonplace of textual organization is that, in the societies of the Christian West, men have enjoyed the privileges of subjectivity and self-representation, while women are positioned as the objects of male sexuality. Thus indexed topics in books and encyclopedias regularly read: "sex: see women"; or "marriage: see women."

My reiteration of the male convention of discussing women in connection with sex seeks not to perpetuate but to display and subvert this placement of women as objects of male desire. It reflects—and reflects *on*—Augustine's own arrangement of women as ancillaries and support systems for both his life and its story. It also problematizes the extent to which the category of the "erotic" has been used simply to mean erotic *for men*. Both Western literature and visual images have represented women as objects of male desire rather than as subjects of a distinctive female sexual desire.[26] It is impossible to glean from Augustine's *Confessions* anything more about each woman who accompanied and supported his life than a few scattered hints about her subjectivity and sexuality. Thus I have chosen to render this aspect of the *Confessions* visible and questionable rather than, for example, attempting to reconstruct the affective timbre of Monica's life from the few details of her childhood, dreams, and reactions that suggest the textual presence of an actual female human being.

There were women in Augustine's life; Augustine recognized and acknowledged that they were formative and central to the structure and shape of that life. Yet their textual "lives," like their actual lives, are lived in Augustine's shadow. Their emotions pale next to the vivid hues and saturation of Augustine's colorful emotions; their ideas never achieve the beauty and profundity of Augustine's, and their actions, no matter how courageous or virtuous, are narrated simply, without the high drama of Augustine's least gestures and actions. An obedient reading of the *Confessions* notices this, recognizing it as a perhaps inevitable by-product of the author's intention to present his own life with candor and subtlety; a disobedient reading, however, questions the author-ized text, fantasizing another text in which the women to whom Augustine was attached might have received simultaneously more flesh and their own souls.

The second matter that deserves brief comment is whether Augustine's sexual orientation can be identified and labelled. He wrote candidly of his attraction to women, of course, but he also acknowledged that no friendship was free of his lust, implying that he was also sexually attracted to men. On the strength of this suggestion, modern readers may be tempted to think of him as bisexual. It is, however, anachronistic in the extreme to attempt to label Augustine's sexual orientation in twentieth-century terms that rely on socially constructed categories. Augustine wrote about bodies and pleasures, not about heterosexuality, homosexuality, or bisexuality. As Michel Foucault, John Boswell, and others have demonstrated, the "homosexual," as a settled sexual preference or orientation, is a relatively recent phenomenon. Male and female homoeroticism, on the other hand, is amply documented throughout the history of the West. We must sacrifice the satisfaction of naming Augustine's sexuality in modern terms, I think, accepting instead his language of multiple bodies and pleasures.

It was a sweet thing to me both to love and to be loved, and more sweet still when I was able to enjoy the body

of my lover. And so I muddied the clear spring of friendship with the dirt of physical desire and clouded over
its brightness with the dark hell of lust. (III.1–2)

Provocatively, Augustine characterizes the Carthage he came to as a young adult as a "hissing caul-
dron of unholy loves."

My soul was in poor health; it burst out into feverish
spots which brought the wretched longing to be
scratched by contact with the objects of sense. . . . It
was a sweet thing to me both to love and to be loved,
and more sweet still when I was able to enjoy the body
of my lover. (III.1)

Documenting his frantic pursuit of strong feeling, tormented by "rods of red-hot iron—the rods of jealousies
and suspicions, fears, angers, and quarrels," Augustine insists in retrospect that he got no pleasure
from erotic experience. He compares his erotic experience to stage plays, in which one participates briefly in
the sufferings of the characters in the play, in that sexual experiences merely "scratched the surface of my
skin. And, as happens after the scratching of poisoned
nails, what came next were feverish swellings, ab-
cesses, and running sores. Such was the life I led. Was
this, my God, a life at all?" (III.2)

The text employs a rhetoric of physical symptoms
to express the violence of erotic desire. The "gaps,
voids, and silences" [27] within Augustine's sexual discourse both stimulate readers' imagination and frustrate their curiosity. After claiming that *no friendship*
was free of his lust, for example, Augustine narrates
the death of a "very dear friend," a young man he had

grown up with, but with whom he discovered a new attachment as a young adult. Heavily judgmental of this friendship at the time of writing, he acknowledges that at the time it was "a friendship that was sweeter to me than all sweetnesses that in this life I had ever known." "I had poured out my soul like water onto sand by loving a man who was bound to die just as if he were an immortal" (IV.8). Yet in the *Confessions'* revisionist history of his experience, Augustine asserts that this relationship did not constitute true friendship "because there can be no true friendship unless those who cling to each other are glued together by you in that love which is spread throughout our hearts by the holy spirit." Augustine acknowledges that, when his friend died,

> My heart was darkened over with sorrow, and whatever I looked at was death. My own country was a torment to me, my own home a strange unhappiness. All those things which we had done and said together became, now that he was gone, sheer torture to me. . . . Only tears were sweet to me, and tears had taken the place of my friend in my heart's love. (IV.4)

Augustine the bishop has a new and exacting standard of friendship that excludes even such an intense friendship as this. In the *Confessions*, there is a profound incommensurability between the passionate experiences of his youth and the interpretation he gave these experiences in early middle age. The reader is tossed between narration and interpretation, forced to fantasize, in the light of her own erotic experience, what she would most like to know about Augustine's sexual relationships and cannot learn from Au-

gustine's severe middle-aged judgment: How did it *feel*
to be an ambitious, high-spirited, amorous young man
in Carthage in the late fourth century?

It is precisely this "unholy" curiosity that Augustine the author attempts to block; the reader's voy-
euristic pleasure in the text must be firmly integrated
and subordinated to Augustine's religious message.
The specifically erotic effect of his narration must not
be permitted to carry the text's weight. Nevertheless,
the unintended effect of Augustine's heavy-handed
control is twofold: the reader's erotic interest is height-
ened by the peepshow effect of his partial—titillating
but unsatisfying—revelations; Augustine's judgmental
interpretation of his sexual relationships provokes the
reader to evoke his own sexual experience in order to
protest Augustine's negative interpretation. Augustine's judgments of his sexual activity sometimes
seem merely silly to the late twentieth-century reader;
sometimes they seem to misrepresent fundamentally
sexual experience, disastrously failing to acknowledge—even while they illustrate—that "the sexual is a
way the soul speaks." [28]

Augustine interprets his sexual activity from the
perspective of a later time, a time he saw as radically
discontinuous with the time of that experience. The
continuity of his life has been abruptly interrupted by
conversion; a new life has emerged: "He who made
us made us anew [*qui fecit refecit*]."[29] In describing
his sexual experience, then, Augustine arouses
readers' erotic interest, but blocks that interest at
the point that it would detract from, rather than
strengthen and intensify, the communication he in-
tends, namely, God's activity in his life. He insists on

the authorial privilege of interpreting his erotic experience himself; at this crucial point, he does not permit the reader the co-authorship he has offered in another context—"anyone can read what I have written and interpret it as he likes" (IX.12). Although Augustine has seduced his readers to energetic subjective engagement with his text, he suddenly demands passive acquiescence to his interpretation. This is perhaps the most frustrating aspect of the *Confessions* for twentieth-century readers.

This one-sided interpretation rings false, not only as a reader questions Augustine's interpretation in the light of her own experience, but also as she considers the perspective of Augustine's sexual partners. For sexual relationship is marked precisely by the impossibility of a unilateral interpretation. *Two* subjectivities are inevitably involved, making erotic experience permanently ambiguous; sexual experience cannot be definitively interpreted from the perspective of only one partner. Whether the erotic activity involves the pleasures of lovemaking or of reading, one of the partners—one lover, one author—cannot define what that experience *was*. One's partner—one's reader—feels, thinks, hears, and reads differently. She inevitably experiences and interprets from a perspective that is different, sometimes even contradictory, to that of the lover/author. That other perspective is inaccessible to the partner unless it is volunteered—even against the grain of the text—by a partner/reader.

The reader learns nothing from the *Confessions* about Augustine's primary partner, the woman who shared his life for thirteen years and who bore their son. Even her name—that initial mark of subjectivity—

is withheld. What did she *feel*, returning to Africa, swearing permanent celibacy, while Augustine chooses a more advantageous marriage? What did she feel, leaving her son—perhaps forever—as she sailed off to her newly solitary existence? Yet it is not the woman, arbitrarily rejected, involuntarily losing her husband of thirteen years and the child of her body, that readers are urged to sympathize with, but Augustine. Augustine, who quickly took another mistress because he could not be alone for the two years until his betrothed was old enough to marry, requires the reader's empathy for his pain in losing her: "Nor was the wound healed which had been made by the cutting off of my previous mistress. It burned, it hurt intensely, and then it festered, and if the pain became duller, it became more desperate" (VI.15). To be sure, Augustine admires his partner's faithfulness and deplores his own slavery to sex, but his pain is vividly present in the text, while hers is totally elided.

Augustine failed to seek to understand and convey the perspectives of others with whom he shared sexual relationships. Moreover, he offers no glimpse of his feelings at the time of the experience, interpreting his sexual activity so negatively that the reader is compelled to wonder why in the world he kept pursuing such dismal and unpleasureable acts. This is exactly what Augustine the author/bishop wants his readers to wonder; the elimination of alternative perspectives— readers' as well as his partners'—produces a didactic text, a text curiously failing to create pleasure exactly at the point of its greatest possibility.

Certainly, an obedient reader finds ample textual justification for this flattening of the complexity and richness of sexual relationship. Augustine insists that sex, for him, was pleasureless because it was compulsive, and acting out compulsions never produces pleasure. Yet the negative rhetoric he uses to describe sexuality—"chains," "hard slavery"—is contradicted by the conventional language of sexual pleasure he is forced to use to designate what he refers to: "It was a sweet thing to me both to love and to be loved, and more sweet still when I was able to enjoy the body of my lover" (III.1). He mentions without giving details: sweetness, delights, desires, voluptuousness. Evidence of sexual delight thus slips through the textual defenses against it, confusing the reader.

Augustine's account of sexual relationship is rendered questionable by his highly selective description of his feelings as they occurred. His memories are dangerous both to author and reader and must be heavily controlled if they are to be represented at all. They are dangerous to Augustine because he has a healthy respect for the durability of compulsive habits, a sense of the fragility of a resolution that is a gift, and therefore not within his control. In a different way, Augustine's memories are also dangerous to readers: if they present sexual experience as attractive, they will provoke imitation. And it is clear that Augustine hopes the reader will learn from his experience, *not* that she will duplicate his experience in order to come to the place of experiential knowledge to which Augustine has come. As pastor, bishop, and spiritual authority, he commits the perennial mistake of parents: he forgets that his present vantage point is the direct and cumulative result of the long process by which he achieved it. He refuses to be aware of the continuity and subjective integrity of his journey, to acknowledge that it was, in fact, by following with the utmost passion a destructive and treacherous path that he came to the emotional bankruptcy which led to a breakthrough. He wants his readers to accept his conclusions without the experience of a similar learning process.

Two interrelated aspects of the *Confessions* as an erotic text remain to be considered. What would it mean, I asked myself in beginning this project, to give a gendered reading of Augustine's *Confessions*? What if I were to refuse the author's positioning of the reader as a male confidant, privy to his subjectivity because temporarily granted—if necessary—an honorary universal (male) subjectivity? Curiously in an erotic text, the *Confessions* tempts the reader to read without a body, especially a female body, to assume the normative male psyche that positions "woman" as object, whether threat or delight. What would I notice if I declined this imputed and infused subjectivity?

We have already remarked on Augustine's seizure of the prerogative of subjectivity in the narration of his separation from his partner of thirteen years. The omission of her perspective, her feelings, from the story he tells is not accidental or incidental. Rather it is a commonplace of Western literature that the subject position be reserved for male subjectivity. Like other great and small texts in this tradition, the *Confessions* places the women with whom Augustine's story is connected as objects, foils for the tale of his physical and psychic development. The absence of female subjectivity in a male autobiography may seem inevitable; I will argue, on the contrary, that our sense of inevitability comes from modern readers' long conditioning to expect that the literary presentation of subjectivity will describe a male subject and assume a male reader. Women readers, in order to become the reader constructed by the text, must read without the female body, assuming the universalized perspective of the male subject. A gendered reading, however, reveals the absence of a female subject position in the text; it also makes visible Augustine's extensive use of male sexuality as a primary and pervasive model for human life. Let us examine each of these results in turn.

We have noticed some aspects of Augustine's presentation of the unnamed woman who was his partner and the mother of their son. She is not, however, the woman most prominently featured in the *Confessions*. That woman is Monica, Augustine's mother. Monica was the woman who accompanied Augustine on his quest for the greatest pleasure from before his birth to his second infancy after his new birth. It was she who followed him—literally and figuratively—through his worldly career to the mystical experience they shared at Ostia just before her death at the age of fifty-six, shortly before Augustine's return to North Africa. It was Monica, Augustine wrote in retrospect, who represented the voice of God to him in his preconversion days in her warnings, pleadings, and tears (II.3).[30] It was she who wept for his salvation—efficacious tears "which fell streaming and watered the ground beneath her eyes in every place where she prayed" (III.11). In Augustine's text, Monica's tears become symbol and literary figure, the crucial connection between "the dirt

of physical desire" with which Augustine was muddied
(III.2) and his ultimate cleansing:

> You saved me, full as I was with the most execrable
> uncleanness, from the waters of the sea and brought
> me to that water of your grace, so that, when I was
> washed in this water, the rivers that flowed from my
> mother's eyes, tears daily shed for me that watered the
> ground below her downcast looks, should be dried up.
> (V.8)

Monica's tears were rewarded by a dream in which
she was told by "a very beautiful young man with a
happy face, smiling at her," that Augustine would one
day stand close to her in faith. Nevertheless, she did
not cease to weep tears that irritated Augustine enormously at the time. She also annoyed Ambrose, who
responded to her pleas to him to remonstrate with the
recalcitrant Augustine: "Now go away and leave me. As
you live, it is impossible that the son of these tears
should perish" (III.12).

Thus far, however, we see through Augustine's
eyes a mother whose story is told only because it reveals important facets of his life. This Monica is the
complete mother, absorbed in her son's career, in planning for his marriage, and in his conversion to Catholic Christianity: "I cannot express how she loved me
and how she labored with much greater pain to give
me birth in the spirit than she had suffered when giving birth to me in the flesh" (V.9). Augustine paints
her relationship with her husband as secondary, pe-
ripheral to her passionate attachment to Augustine.
And, as Augustine presents her in the *Confessions*,

she has no interest in her other children, though we know that Augustine had a brother and a sister.

It was in Monica's company also that Augustine experienced the most intense pleasure of his early adulthood. Alone together, Augustine and Monica lean out a window overlooking a garden, discussing heaven, "and very sweet our talk was." Trying to imagine the joys of heaven, they began by thinking of "the greatest possible delights of our bodily senses," only to pass on, with burning affections, step by step, from material things to eternal wisdom, "meditating and speaking and looking with wonder at your works."

> As we talked, yearning toward this wisdom, we did, with the whole strength of our heart's impulse, just lightly come into touch with [wisdom]. (IX.10)

Immediately after this experience, Monica professes "no longer to find any pleasure in this life," her greatest earthly pleasure having been to see Augustine also "despise the pleasures of this world." Now that Augustine has, with Monica's help, resolved the question of how to get—and keep—the greatest pleasure, Monica is free to die; she had given him both physical and spiritual birth.

In spite of the tenderness, unstinting appreciation, and terrible loss Augustine felt for Monica after her death, the *Confessions* is his story, a story in which Monica plays the supporting role to which he assigns her. Even her death becomes an occasion for his scrupulous analysis of his own feelings:

> I was deeply vexed that these human feelings should have such power over me—though in the proper order

and lot of the human condition these things must be—
and I grieved at my grief with a new grief and so was
consumed with a double sorrow. (IX.12)

Is this the Augustine whose copious weeping, duly reported, had marked so many important moments in
his life—the death of his unnamed friend (IV.4) and his
conversion (VIII.12), to name only the most prominent? Tears are significant to Augustine; he pauses in
narrating his most intense experiences to analyze
them: "why is it that tears are sweet to us when we are
unhappy?" Augustine is not ashamed to acknowledge
that tears can be pleasurable; they reveal the soul's
attachments: "How is it that from the bitterness of life
we can pluck such sweet fruit in mourning and weeping and sighing and lamentation?" (IV.5) At the time
of Monica's death, however, he thinks that tears are
theologically incorrect since Monica has died as a faithful Christian, in the hope of resurrection, so that, in
fact, "she was not altogether dead." Yet it *is* still the
case that "Now that I had lost the great comfort of her,
my soul was wounded and my life was, as it were, torn
apart, since it had been a life made up of hers and
mine together" (IX.12). Augustine has used these same
expressions in describing the death of his dear friend
("I felt that my soul and my friend's had been one soul
in two bodies" [IV.6]), and his separation from his partner of thirteen years ("the woman with whom I was in
the habit of sleeping was torn from my side" VI.15).

Augustine finally finds what he considers a valid
reason for grief; he weeps, not primarily for Monica,
who is safe with God, but for himself:

And now suddenly I had lost all this. . . . With you
seeing me I found solace in weeping for her and for

myself, on her behalf and on my own. So I allowed the tears, which I had been holding back to fall, and I let them flow as they would, making them a pillow for my heart, and my heart rested on them. (IX.12)

Augustine still fears a judgmental reader who "despises" him for weeping thus for the loss of his mother, so he concludes by begging his readers to weep rather for Augustine's sins and to pray for his parents' sins, "that as many as shall read this may remember at your altar Monica, your servant, with Patricius, her husband, through whose flesh you brought me into this life, though how I do not know" (IX.13).

There is, however, another Monica in Augustine's account, a Monica who comes close to being the subject of her own experience. In relating her death, Augustine begins to think of her life and to recall stories she had told him about her childhood and her marriage. We glimpse Monica as a young girl who stole gulps of wine from the family casks until one day a maid shamed her into ceasing to indulge this "excessive fondness for wine" by calling her a drunkard (IX.8). We see her as a young wife, admired by her friends for her skill at handling an irascible mother-in-law and an unfaithful husband with a bad temper. She managed to avoid the domestic violence prevalent in her society by "patience and forbearance": "there were many wives with husbands much milder than hers who went about with their faces disfigured by the marks of blows" (IX.9). These quick sketches of the life of a North African middle-class woman, however, give less of a sense of Monica's subjectivity than of her son's fond but highly selective memories of her.

Vignettes of Monica's life serve to demonstrate her selfless servanthood, first to her husband "whom she served as her master" (IX.6), and finally to Augustine, his son, and his friends. In a moment of honesty that most readers of the *Confessions* have thought of as a charming tribute rather than a statement of fact, Augustine asks himself: "What comparison was there between the respect I paid to her and the slavery she offered to me?" (IX.12) As a daughter of Eve, Monica models the position of suffering assigned to women in the pain with which she gave Augustine physical and spiritual birth (V.8). She crystallizes the figure of the good woman, the nourishing, weeping mother who devotes herself entirely to the good of her son.

There is another female figure in the *Confessions*—the seductive, dangerous woman who distracts Augustine from his pursuit of true pleasures. He invoked "that bold woman in the allegory of Solomon" as a representation of the bodily senses when he described his misguided search for God among the objects of sense:

> She it was who seduced me, for she found my soul dwelling out of doors, in the eye of my flesh, and chewing over in myself the cud of what I had eaten through that eye. (III.6)

Augustine's description in book 8 of his conversion in the garden at Milan incorporates both of these female figures, the good mother and the tempting seductress, to dramatize his spiritual crisis. While Augustine is pushed and pulled in the slippery battle between his two wills, his former "mistresses" pluck at his sleeve and whisper in his ear, invoking the strong grip of habit as they murmured softly, "Do you think that you can live without us?" (VIII.11) In the midst of this struggle, another female figure appears: Continence, calm and serene, cheerful without wantonness, full of chaste dignity "was enticing me to come to her without hesitation, stretching out to receive and to embrace me with those holy hands of hers."

Continence approaches Augustine surrounded by women and men, boys and girls of every age who followed her. Augustine uses the language of seduction to describe her effect on him: smiles, encouragement, enticement, embrace—a counter seduction to that of the "toys and trifles, utter vanities." Continence is a mother; her allurement is not that of a sexual tease, but she attracts him with the maternal reassurance that he will receive help if he chooses her. "The Lord, her husband," the true father, will support and sustain those who choose to yield to her:

> Why do you try and stand by yourself, and so not stand at all? Let him support you. Do not be afraid. He will not draw away and let you fall. Put yourself fearlessly in his hands. He will receive you and will make you well. (VIII.11)

These female figures with their alternative seductions personify the crisis of Augustine's conversion. The mother, Continence, won. Augustine's conversion was to continence, as he had known it must be.

Conversion to continence, so compelling to upwardly mobile men of Augustine's class and education in the late fourth century, needs to be very carefully interpreted in relation to Augustine's literary treatment of women. Augustine gives several examples of such conversions in the *Confessions*, examples that,

as he acknowledges, cumulatively inspired his own decision. At the end of the fourth century, monasteries,
in which communties lived "a way of life that was full
of the sweet fragrance of [God]" (VIII.6), offered a new
and exciting lifestyle. Augustine reports his amazed
excitement on hearing for the first time of a monastery
"full of good brothers" right outside the walls of Milan
and under the supervision of Ambrose. The sudden,
about-face, complete conversion of life to such a community captured the imagination of men like Augustine. They were eager to report to one another yet
another such conversion.

A strong element of male bonding, loyalty, and
friendship can be seen in these decisions. Referring
to a male friend, Augustine gives his formula for true
friendship: "Those who cling together in love are glued
together by [God] in that love which is spread throughout our hearts by the holy spirit which is given to us"
(IV.4). Shortly before Augustine's own conversion, Ponticianus related to Augustine the conversion story of
two young men, both of them engaged to be married,
who decided instead to enter the full-time religious life
as "comrades in so great a service and for so great a
reward." The women to whom they were engaged,
when they heard what had happened, imitated them,
dedicating their virginity to God (VIII.6).

In the *Confessions*, Augustine and his friends repeatedly construe the love of women as incompatible
with committed love of God. The passionate commitment of like-minded men to the mutual and communal
pursuit of the knowledge and love of God, on the other
hand, is understood as the perfect form for the search.
Presumably, sexual activity in the first relationship,

and its sublimation in the second, makes the difference, though Augustine does not say so directly. In any case, he apparently has no fear of the "glue of love" when it connects his life with that of another man, but he cannot imagine loving a woman in a relationship in which each partner supported, encouraged, and provoked the other to self-knowledge and spiritual progress.

Continence in male community was to become the pattern of Augustine's new life. Alypius, his friend, had shared—at a slight distance—the storm of Augustine's conversion to continence: "when he was there I still felt myself in privacy" (VIII.8). He would also be baptized with Augustine and with Augustine's son, Adeodatus. Together Augustine and Alypius brought up Adeodatus "in your discipline" (IX.6). Originally, about ten young men had planned to form a community, some of them having the necessary wealth to make possible the leisured life of philosophical conversation they anticipated. There were problems with this plan, however, as some of the company were married and their wives protested. "And so the whole scheme, which had been so well worked out, fell to pieces in our hands and was abandoned as impracticable" (VI. 14).

A more workable community formed after Augustine's conversion. In preparation for their baptism, Augustine, Adeodatus, and Alypius, joined by Evodius and served by Monica, retired to a country estate near Milan at Cassiciacum owned by another friend, Verecundus, a Milanese professor. They expected soon to be joined by Nebridius, who would be baptized shortly after them, but who died before he could join them. Upon returning to Milan to be baptized, the company "stayed together with the intention of finding a place to live together in the good life which we planned" (VI.14; IX.8). They decided to return to Africa and had traveled as far as the seaport of Ostia when Monica died.

Verecundus is a good example of the fascination with conversion to continence that permeated Augustine's Milanese society. Verecundus, not yet himself a Christian, wanted to become a Christian and join Augustine and his company at Cassiciacum. But he was married. Even though his wife was a Christian, Augustine writes, "she was a fetter which clung to him more tightly than all the rest, preventing him from setting out on the journey on which we had started" (IX.3). And Verecundus would "not be a Christian in any other way except the way that was impossible to him." However, Verecundus suddenly became ill while his friends were at Cassiciacum and was baptized on his deathbed. Verecundus's story reveals that a conversion to continence was understood both as a rejection of emotional and sexual relationship with women and as a commitment to male community. Augustine himself discarded both his profession and his engagement in choosing a life of male companionship, a life which contained, he says, "wonderful sweetness" (IX.6).

The actual women Augustine described in the *Confessions* circulate between the female figures of his text. Monica is on the side of Continence, the "fruitful mother of children," a woman only in her "woman's clothing." Augustine writes that she had a "masculine faith"; she was "tranquil in her age, maternal in her love, Christian in her goodness" (IX.4). His partner in sexual relationship, however, stood close to the "mistresses" that pluck at his sleeve and whisper in his ear, holding him back from commitment to continence. Through no fault of her own, she is tainted by her role as the object of his slavery to the "need for a woman" (VIII.1).

Nevertheless, Augustine never explicitly blamed his partner for what he recognized as his own sexual addiction; he mentions no attempts on her part to seduce or to hold onto him. On the contrary, according to his own report she seems to accept his decisions without question or opposition, even when she is rejected. Her textual absence as subject of her own experience, however, is at least partly the result of Augustine's association of her with his rejected sexuality. Even her motherhood does not modify Augustine's identification of her with sex. Her motherhood, Augustine says, was an incidental result of their sexual activity:

> With her I learned by my own experience how great a difference there is between the self-restraint of the marriage covenant which is entered into for the sake of having children, and the mere pact made between two people whose love is lustful and who do not want to have children—even though, if children are born, they compel us to love them. (IV.2)

Augustine refuses to picture his partner as a mother, referring to their child as "the son I had from her [*ex illa*]" (VI.15). Yet I cannot help wondering if the jealous infant Augustine observed at its mother's breast (I.6) was not his own son, Adeodatus, the child he would have had the most opportunity to observe. In any case, he gives no sketches of this woman in her role of motherhood, maintaining her in the role of his sexual partner.

There are, in the *Confessions*, seductive female figures; there are no seductive women. It is important to notice that Augustine fully claims and takes responsibility for his sexual lust; this is remarkable, given the long literary tradition of male projection of sexual temptation onto women. Nevertheless, his understanding and literary treatment of actual women is limited by the female figures that inhabit his psyche: the good mother and the sexual object. A gendered reading of the *Confessions* reveals that it contains no depictions of women who, like Augustine, suffer and struggle to define and achieve their own goals.

We have seen that Augustine's body—its feeling, movements, and gestures—provided him with an observable and accurate key to the condition of his soul. We must now examine more carefully the significance of continence, the rejection of sexual activity, for Augustine. Throughout the *Confessions*, Augustine employs juxtaposed images of himself as alternatively distracted and dispersed among transitory pleasures or gathered and collected by a disciplined "return" to himself and thus to God. His most concentrated description of these alternatives occurs in XI.29:

> I have been spilled and scattered among times whose order I do not know; my thoughts, the innermost bowels of my soul, are torn apart with the crowding tumults of variety, and so it will be until all together I can flow into you, purified and molten by the fire of your love.

Continence is, on the one hand, as we have seen, a literal practice, a positive commitment to renouncing sexual activity. It is also, however, symbolic for Augustine, of a unified and unifying affection and attention.

The project of writing the *Confessions* was itself simultaneously an exercise for Augustine in re-collecting himself and in reviewing, renaming, and reconstructing his life. It was, in the most literal sense of the phrase, a "talking cure," the final stage of a long process of conversion:

> I want to call back to mind my past impurities and the carnal corruptions of my soul, not because I love them, but so that I may love you, my God. It is for the love of your love that I do it, going back over those most wicked ways of mine in the bitterness of my recollection so that the bitterness may be replaced by the sweetness of you, O unfailing sweetness, happy sweetness and secure! And gathering myself together from the scattered fragments into which I had been broken and dissipated during all that time when, being turned away from you, the One, I lost myself in the distractions of the many. (II.1)

Augustine continuously juxtaposes verbs that suggest a hemorrhage of vital energy with those that indicate an arrest of that flow, a collection or gathering back of the wasted spill. "Sorrows, confusions, and mistakes" (I.20) were the immediate result of the scattered self; the long-term effects were even more pernicious: starvation, poor health, wounds, and fever (III.1). Augustine did not imagine the "self" assumed by most twentieth-century people, an individual self whose existence is guaranteed and bounded by a body.

Augustine's "self" or "inner man" is, rather, a mini-
mally differentiated subject constructed and defined by
its flow of energy, differentiated only by the objects of
its attention and affection. Its fluid and determinative
energy might flow in one of two opposite directions:
either toward objects in the sensible world or toward
God, the source of its being.

Augustine describes concupiscence, a nondiscrim-
inating grasping at objects that cross one's path in the
anxiety that something will be missed, as a consistent
human pattern of behavior from infancy to adulthood
and old age. No one, Augustine writes categorically,
"can be continent unless [God] gives it" (X.31). Conversion consists, then, not only in arresting this outward
flow of the soul's essence, but also in a thorough and
systematic recollection of the scattered self. The self
that has been dispersed—draped—on an ever-shifting
kaleidoscope of slippery sensible objects must be gathered: "I was tossed here and there, spilled on the
ground, scattered abroad; I boiled over in my fornica-
tions." In this vivid passage, Augustine directly contrasts women's embraces with God's embraces: he
should have listened to his mother's warnings, he says,
and waited for God's embraces. Instead, he "boiled up
and ran troubled along the course of my own stream."
He concedes that an early marriage might have put his
sexual activity to a worthy use: "then the waves of my
youth might have spent themselves on the shore of
marriage . . . in the purposeful begetting of children"
(II.2). As it was, however, no limit was placed on "the
fleeting beauties of these new temptations."

Augustine's metaphors of tumescence contribute
to the cumulative connotations by which he estab-

lishes male sexuality as his model of scattered and wasted strength. He consistently used the verbs *turgeo* and *tumeo* to describe the "swelling" or "swollen" condition of prideful arrogance that was his settled style (III.3, 5). "I was separated from you by the swelling (*tumor*) of my pride. It was as though my cheeks had swollen up so that I could not see out of my eyes" (VII.7). Swelling led to spilling: "I was very pleased with myself and swelling with arrogance . . . I was given free play with no kind of severity to control me and was allowed to dissipate myself in all kinds of ways" (II.3).

> And I asked: "What is wickedness?" and found that it is not a substance but a perversity of the will turning away from you, God, . . . toward lower things—casting away, as it were, its own insides, and swelling with desire for what is outside it. (VII.16)

The affective state of such scatteredness, Augustine insists, is lassitude, restlessness, weariness, depression, and dejection (II.7).

The first contrast between God and men that Augustine remarks on at the beginning of the *Confessions* is God's capacity for filling all things without dispersion or diminution: "When you are poured out over us, it is not you who are brought low but us who are raised up, not you who are scattered, but us who are brought together" (I.3). Augustine, however, has learned through experience that he must practice continence if he is not to be "spilled on the ground." Gathering, containing, recollecting: these are the activities that must replace dissipation—*both literally and symbolically.* Continence was, for Augustine, the essential pivot on which he turned—returned—to God:

The Word itself calls you to come back . . . you will lose
nothing. What is withered in you will flower again, and
all your illnesses will be made well, and all that was
flowing and wasting from you will regain shape and
substance and will form part of you again. (IV.11)

"You will lose nothing"; Augustine describes himself as replacing, through continence, the "drunkenness" of undifferentiated lust "for honors, for money,
for marriage" (VI.6), with "intoxication" [31] with God-
given pleasure: "Oh, that you would come into my
heart and so inebriate it that I would forget my own
evils and embrace my one and only good, which is you!"
(I.5) Clearly, Augustine's idea of continence is not that
of an austere renunciation of delights, but their direct
exchange for greater, more trustworthy, lasting delights. Indeed, even the beauties of the world can be
enjoyed only by the one who is not enslaved to them
because "a slave can't enjoy that to which he is enslaved." Augustine lists some "objects of beauty and
worth" that can be enjoyed—even "followed"—"if human beings do so in such a way as not to depart from
God." His examples include: beautiful bodies, gold, sil-
ver, the sense of touch, all senses, worldly honor, life
itself, and human friendship (II.5).

Augustine's early prayer, "Make me continent but
not yet" (VIII.7) has been answered. His sexual activity
ceased after the conversion of his will. After this compulsive expenditure of vital energy has been arrested,
he directs his attention to more minor, less enervating
losses. He scrutinizes his eating habits, love of music,
idle curiosity, and "temptations of the eyes." Even
though these milder attachments are far less debilitating than sex for Augustine, they are potentially perni-

cious in that they cause small but cumulative leaks of his recollection. For example:

> Placed as I am among these temptations, I strive every day against this concupiscence in eating and drinking; for this is not the sort of thing that I can decide to give up once and for all and never touch again, as I was able to do with sex. (X.31)

Throughout his extended discussion of the pleasures of the senses in book 10, Augustine repeatedly invokes his settled formula: the objects of the senses, good in themselves, are potentially triggers for concupiscence and therefore not "among things of little importance." "You command us to be continent. Give what you command, and command what you will," he repeats, over and over (X.37). Anything at all at which "we greedily snatch" removes a person from "planning our joy in your truth" (X.36).

Continence, as we have seen, was the key to changing not only the course of Augustine's life but also the direction of his longing and passion. Continence was, on the one hand, a literal practice, a positive commitment to abstaining from sexual activity. As a practice it was, for Augustine, I emphasize, not an inactivity, a *not* doing. It was quite literally a *practice*, simultaneously a gathering and centering of the self and an energetic resistance. But continence was more than a practice for Augustine. It was also symbolic of a unified and unifying affection and attention, and thus continence defined the form and dynamic of the spiritual life for Augustine and, because of the strength and beauty of his description, for Western Christianity in general.

In Augustine's physical and spiritual universe, the hoarding of seminal fluid became the practice and paradigm for an integrated life, a life which, by any human measurement, was successful and enormously productive, not least in the seminal writings that flowed from his pen. In demonstrating the physical base of Augustine's spirituality, my intention is not to discredit or minimize his description of the dynamic of the spiritual life. It is rather to understand the recollected life as one form of spirituality, not the only, or the necessary, structure.

As his own discussion demonstrates, Augustine was well aware of the danger of his construction of spirituality; he knew that he must *keep* insisting that no disparagement of objects—good in themselves, the good creation of a good Creator—is intended. Yet it was the dynamic of temptation and resistance he described so forcefully that has captured the attention of generations of Christians rather than his disclaimer of any scorn for sensual objects.[32] Augustine's formulation of the spiritual life as a withdrawal from attachment to the world of senses and objects has played a role in creating the present condition of the earth, a planet in ecological and nuclear crisis.

I do not want to discuss at length the vexed question of whether, or how much, a historical author can be blamed for concepts that can be shown to have proven destructive in their institutional effects. Yet, because Augustine is perhaps the historical author most often targeted for blame for myriad destructive effects in Western societies, it is important to comment briefly on these accusations. On the one hand, it is a cheap shot to blame historical authors for effects that are observable only from the vantage point of another time and place. No author can fully predict the forms that the influence and institutionalization of her ideas will take; she should of course endeavor to do so, but her primary attention is inevitably directed to the constraints of her own historical location. On the other hand, the effects as well as the carefully stipulated intentions of the author need to be a part of the evaluation of the present usefulness of historical ideas. It is ultimately the passivity—the intellectual and practical laziness—of generations of Christians who adopted Augustine's formulations without discernment of their concrete effects within their societies that is to be blamed for the destructive effects of Augustine's ideas.

To recognize Augustine's conception of spirituality as based on his own most intimate physical experience, then, is not to discount it, but rather to reveal its touching poignancy, its fragility, and its contingency. It is also to urge that other models of spirituality be imagined, fleshed out, and bodied forth. Alternative models are desperately needed, models that respond to the crises of our own day by emphasizing attention to, and affection for, the vulnerable and threatened earth, by energizing committed labor for peace and justice, and by illuminating the spiritual discipline of loving relationship and community.

4

Textual Harassment: The God's-Eye View

*Delight orders the soul
. . . where the soul's
delight is, there is its
treasure.*[33]

*The soul feeds on that
in which it finds joy.*[34]

Augustine's practice of continence radically changed his way of seeing the world. Stopping the outward rush of physical and psychic energy, he was released from the tyranny of objects and centered *intus* (inside). A discerning, evaluating, choosing will, a *free* will—"suddenly called forth in a moment"—directs his life. Former pleasures spontaneously lose their attraction and are exchanged for ultimate sweetness:

> How sweet it suddenly became to me to be without the sweetness of those empty toys! How glad I was to give up the things I had been so afraid to lose! For you cast them out from me, you true and supreme sweetness; you cast them out and you entered into me to take their place, sweeter than all pleasure . . . brighter than all light, but more inward than all hidden depths. (IX.1)

Contrary to twentieth-century psychoanalytic theory, insight follows behavioral change; altered *practice* creates converted perspective.

In book 10, then, Augustine's agenda changes: he moves from confessing "not what I once was, but what I now am." "There are many people who want to know this—both those who know me personally and those who do not" (X.3). Augustine is aware of being a public figure, a man who has attracted popular interest, as Victorinus, the Roman professor of rhetoric described in VIII.2, had before him. Again he specifies his ideal reader; he asks for

> a brotherly mind which is glad for me when it sees good in me and sorry for me when it sees bad in me, because, whether it sees good or bad, it loves me. It is to people like this that I shall show myself. (X.4)

Augustine's understanding of his past and present experience coalesced in images of concupiscence and continence. At present, he is collected, gathered, no longer spilled and scattered. He no longer loses energy and vitality—like seminal fluid—on the pursuit of sex, power, and possessions. He now contains himself, ordered around a strong central pleasure. His security, however, is fragile; it relies on God's gift: "no one can be continent unless you give it" (X.31).

All my hope is nowhere except in your great mercy.
Grant us what you command, and command us what
you will. You demand that we should be continent . . .
it is by continence that we are brought together and
brought back to the One, after having dissipated ourselves among the many (X.29).

Augustine's reliance on God has a tensile and trustworthy strength that could never be the result of his
own fierce determination and "will power." Augustine's
pleasure in continence is the firmest guarantor of his
perserverence: "O love, ever burning, and never extin-
guished, charity, my God, set me on fire!" he exclaims
immediately after he describes the psychodynamics of
continence.

Still, he confesses, "I do not know in my case what
temptations I can and what I cannot resist" (X.5). He
has renounced sexual activity:

You commanded me to abstain from sleeping with a
mistress, and with regard to marriage you advised me
to take a better course than the one that you permitted
me. And since you gave me the power, it was done.
(X.30)

Nevertheless, some minor but unsettling fissures in
Augustine's continence trouble him. Memory retains
images of former pleasures, firmly bonded "on my soul"
and "in my flesh" by long habit. These images are inef-
fective during the day, but at night they sometimes
emerge in their full strength and vividness. When he
is asleep, "they not only cause pleasure but go so far
as to obtain assent and something very like reality."
Augustine feels himself the helpless victim of these
nocturnal experiences which seem to him to be inde-
pendent of his psyche, occurring only in his flesh: "it

was not we who did something which was, to our re-
gret, somehow or other done in us" (X.30).

There are also pleasures which cannot be given up
"once and for all, and never touched again, as I was
able to do with sex." Food and drink are ongoing neces-
sities, but it is also "sweet to me, and I fight against
this sweetness so that I shall not become its prisoner"
(X.31). Overeating, he confesses "has sometimes crept
up on your servant," and he experiences "a dangerous
kind of pleasure." Nervously, Augustine itemizes his
present temptations to concupiscence of the various
senses—hearing, smell, vision—confessing that "it is
not easy for me to give them exactly the right place"
(X.33). Fluctuating between the "danger of pleasure"
and "the error of being too severe," Augustine experiences the inevitable dilemna of a fixation on control.
He has become a "question to myself," all his senses
and their pleasures constantly problematized; if he
yields to a "pleasurable relaxation" of vigilance, he risks
"the concupiscence of the flesh which is present in the
delight we take in all the pleasures of the senses"
(X.35). He thinks of himself as walking in an "enormous forest, full of snares and dangers" (X.35).

Sight—the "pleasure of the eyes"—is an especially
volatile sense: the eyes love beautiful shapes of all
kinds,

> glowing and delightful colors. These things must not
> take hold on my soul; that is for God to do. . . . These
> things affect me during all the time every day that I am
> awake. (X. 34)

With extraordinary sensual sensitivity, Augustine recognizes his dependence on light: "if light is suddenly

withdrawn, I look for it again with longing, and if it is absent for long, my mind grows sad." Employing a conventional literary device and remembering his own erotic experience, he figures light, the "queen of colors," as a seductress: "she glides up to me in shape after shape, cajoling me . . . she makes her way forcibly into my mind." Compared to incorporeal light—"light itself"—corporeal light is "a tempting and dangerous sweetness, like a sauce spread over the life of this world for its blind lovers." He mixes metaphors, but the message is clear: the project cannot be to attempt to live in physical darkness, but immediately to carry enjoyment of physical light "up to God" so that he is not "carried away by it into spiritual sleep" (X.34).

The objects of the senses must remain in permanent ambiguity for Augustine; they can be neither rejected nor entirely affirmed. Despite their capacity to seduce, "outer beauties" signal the presence of the great beauty, beauty itself. Only the disciplined and discerning eye can see the "invisible light" at the heart of visble light. Augustine concludes his scrutiny of the dangerous pleasures of the senses by suggesting daringly that the pleasures of the physical senses can be contiguous with the spiritual senses. In fact, they provide the most accurate and precise analogy for the greatest pleasure, enjoyment of beauty itself:

> Late it was that I loved you, beauty so ancient and so new, late have I loved you! And see, you were within me and I was outside, and there I sought for you and in my ugliness I plunged into the beauties that you have made. You were with me and I was not with you. Those outer beauties kept me far from you, yet if they had not been in you, they would not have existed at all. You

called, you cried out, you shattered my deafness: you flashed, you shone, you scattered my blindness: you breathed perfume, and I drew in my breath and I pant for you: I tasted, and I am hungry and thirsty: you touched me and I burned for your peace. (X.27)

The necessary practice and attitude for the conversion of *foris* (outside) into *intus* (inside) is continence. Outer beauty can be gathered into the recollected person and transformed into concrete instances of the great beauty, beauty itself. The later books of the *Confessions* describe a converted world of senses and objects, reformed by the disciplined eye of the continent Augustine. The "whole torrent" of Augustine's love and longing is carried in one great stream that flows toward God:

Now my good things were not external and were not sought with the eyes of the flesh in this sun that we see. For those who find their joys in things outside easily become vain and waste themselves on things seen and temporal and, with their minds starving, go licking at shadows. Oh that they would grow tired of their lack of nourishment. . . . If only they could see the eternal light inside themselves. For it was there, there in the place where I had been angry with myself, inside, in my own room, there where I had been pierced . . . there it was that you began to grow sweet to me. (IX.4)

Augustine has identified the psychic place at which the converted self is constituted. He now explores the structure and contours of this "place" and the self that occupies it. Memory is both a container and an activity. As a container, Augustine pictures memory alternatively as the "stomach of the mind"

(X.14) or as "fields and spacious palaces" (X.8). It is a "treasure house" containing more than one would ever want to remember, so that when memories come crowding, too thick and fast for perusal, Augustine must "brush some of them away with the hand of my heart, until the thing that I want is discovered." Memory can gather the experiences, feelings, thoughts, and sensations of a lifetime and run through them discursively.

Augustine describes the activity of remembering and organizing one's memories as an important kind of re-collection:

> By the act of thought we are, as it were, collecting together things which the memory did contain, though in a disorganized and scattered way, and by giving them our close attention we are arranging for them to be as it were stored up ready to hand in that same memory where they lay hidden, neglected, and dispersed. . . . In fact what one is doing is collecting them from their dispersal. (X.11)

In fact, "memory itself is mind" (X.14). Augustine marvels at the power of memory: "It is something terrifying, my God, a profound and infinite multplicity; and this thing is the mind, and this thing is I myself" (X.17).

Yet the memory does not contain Augustine's "true life"; to reach that, he must "go past this force of mine called memory. . . . I mount up *through my mind* toward you" (X.17). To seek true life is to seek God, Augustine says, and to seek God is not to seek a substance or entity, but to seek the happy life (X.20). The happy life, Augustine concludes, is to be discovered in memory: "for we could not love it if we did not know it." It is recollected and reconstructed in the memory of the joys that occur in every person's life.

This concept is an important one for Augustine. The happy life cannot be experienced vicariously; rather, an idea of the happy life must be collected from memories of individual personal joy, vividly experienced. *Any joys will do*, "base joys and disgraceful things," as well as "good and worthy" joys (X.21). Augustine finds, in the universality of longing for the happy life, evidence that joys of some sort occur in every person's life: "Is not the happy life the thing that all people desire, literally every single person without exception?" (X.20) In other writings he insists in great detail on the universality of this longing, saying in one sermon that even the person who hangs himself does so because he expects to be happier in death than in life. Memories of happiness, because of their universality, are normative.

The recollection of all kinds of personal joy is the first requirement, the *method*, the necessary disciplined commitment: "For me, Lord, certainly this is hard labor, hard labor inside myself, and I have become to myself a piece of difficult ground, not to be worked over without much sweat" (X.16). Ultilmately, however, it is not the memory of any old joys that enables the happy life, but joy in truth: "certainly the happy life is joy in you, who are truth" (X.23). But joy in truth, Augustine labors to establish, can also claim a sort of universality. Just as every person longs for happiness, everyone can be said to love truth; even those who intend to deceive others do not wish themselves to be deceived:

> This human mind of ours, so blind and sick, so foul and ill-favored, wants to be hidden itself, but hates to have anything hidden from it. . . . Wretched as it is, it prefers to find joy in truth than in falsehoods. (X.23)

If both longing for the happy life and a preference for truth are universal, why is it so notoriously difficult for human beings to achieve the happy life?

> Because they are more strongly taken up by other things which have more power to make them unhappy than that, which they so dimly remember, has to make them happy. (X.23)

It takes committed effort to hold onto one's memories of joy and longing for the happy life; happiness is a discipline as well as a gift. Receiving from God is not a passive, but a strenuously active experience: "For there is still only a little light in people, and they must walk, yes, they must walk, that the darkness overtake them not" (X.23).

But Augustine tires of recounting the story of his exterior and interior life. His "pen's tongue" fatigues; the "drops of time" available to him are too precious; "the moments fly past" (XI.2). He prefers to meditate and reflect on the scriptures. In scripture, the voice of the pages is God's voice: "See, your voice is my joy; your voice surpasses all abundance of pleasures." Augustine changes his content and style in book 11 for the sake of his own pleasure and "to stir up my own and my readers' devotion" (XI.1). He begins to comment on the first chapters of Genesis: "I want to hear and I want to understand how 'in the beginning you made heaven and earth'" (XI.3).

And now Augustine's writing is threaded with self-assurance: "I know this . . . I know it . . . and everyone else knows it as I do. . . . We know, Lord, we know it" (XI.7). He is as sure about God's changelessness as he was unsure, in book 10, about his own shifting motivations. He understands scripture by divine illumination: "What is that light that shines through me and strikes my heart without hurting it? And I am both terrified and set on fire" (XI.9).

Emboldened by this hermeneutical privilege, Augustine endeavors to explain time, an ambitious undertaking, one that cannot be accomplished by the unaided light of a "fluttering mind." Even with divine illumination, it is not long before Augustine acknowledges: "I am asking questions, Father, not making statements" (XI.17):

> What then is time? I know what it is if no one asks me what it is; but if I want to explain it to someone who has asked me, I find that I do not know. (XI.14)

Gradually, however, Augustine works his way into seeing "perfectly clearly"

> that neither the future nor the past are in existence, and that it is incorrect to say that there are three times—past, present, and future. Though one might perhaps say: "There are three times, a present of things past, a present of things present, and a present of things future." (XI.20)

Yet this understanding is only a temporary solace; after a lengthy discussion, he confesses himself in "a bad

state indeed," perplexed because he cannot even identify "what it is that I do not know" (XI.25).

Augustine ponders the structure of time with intense fascination; he seeks to understand this philosophical   question   with   the   same   passionate
engagement that earlier he had sought to understand
his own actions and feelings. He is in a state of excitement:

> My soul is on fire to solve this very complicated enigma
> . . . let my longing penetrate into these things. . . .
> Grant me what I love; for I do love it and it was you who
> granted me to love. . . . By Christ I beg you, in his
> name, the holy of holies, let no one disturb me. (XI. 22)

Clearly, the quality of his own involvement has bridged
the change in content from narrative autobiography
to philosophical reflection. The curiosity over "things
which it does no good to know and which men only
want to know for the sake of knowing" (X.35), which
he had previously condemned so vociferously, seems to
have reappeared in another guise. Troubled by his own
penchant for distraction—by gossip or by such slight
spontaneous entertainments as a dog chasing a hare—
Augustine now can rationalize philosophical curiosity
as "contemplating the delights of the Lord" (XI.22).

He seeks an enabling analogy for explaining time's
extension; he experiments with music, with the movements of bodies, and with spoken language, which—
aha!—resembles "the whole of a human life" in that as
it proceeds further and further, "the expectation grows
shorter and the memory grows longer" (XI.28). And Augustine has found the perfect analogy for time: human
life. A life, extended over a long period, is like a person

who is disseminated—extended and distended—
among transitory objects:

> My life is a kind of distraction and dispersal. And thy
> right hand upheld me in my Lord . . . the Mediator be-
> tween thee, the One, and us, the many (many also in
> our many distractions over so many things), . . . that I
> may be gathered up from my former days to follow the
> One, . . . not wasted and scattered on things which are
> to come and things which will pass away, but in-
> tent. . . . But I have been spilled and scattered among
> times whose order I do not know; my thoughts, the
> innermost bowels of my soul, are torn in pieces with
> the crowding tumults of variety, and so it will be until
> all together I can flow into you, purified and liquified
> by the fire of your love. (XI.29; see also XII.10)

In his excitement, Augustine piles one metaphor on
another. His primary metaphor is that of continence;
he juxtaposes being "spilled and scattered" with being
"gathered up." Yet in the next sentence, another prop-
erty of liquid than the capacity to be spilled occurs to
him, and he begs to be liquified and poured into the
changeless God, there to "stand and become set in you,
in my mold, in your truth" (XI.30).

He has found what he sought—not, after all, philosophical understanding, but the "healed eye" by which
he can "share the joy of your light," an immutably eternal knowledge in which he can, by God's gift, participate. By investing his own "fluttering mind" in that of
the "truly eternal creator of minds," Augustine enjoys
a stability, a permanent security that has become his
central requirement for true pleasure. Humility, inspired by a realistic recognition of "the neediness of
my life" and the opposite of prideful inflation, is the

requisite human stance for receptivity: "the humble in heart are the house in which you dwell. For you raise up those who are bowed down; you are their height and from that height they do not fall" (XI.31).

*
* *

In book 12, Augustine also describes creation on the model of continence, a gathering and shaping of previously created invisible and formless matter into the beautiful "earth I tread on and the earth I wear" (XII.2). His attempt to contemplate a genuinely form-less matter—not simply grotesque bodies with inter-changeable parts—fills him with anxiety because it makes him recall vividly his own earlier formlessness:

> I flowed downward and I was in the dark, but even from there, even from there I loved you. . . . I heard your voice behind me, calling me back, and I could scarcely hear it for all the noise made by those without your peace. And now, look, I return thirsty and panting to your fountain. Let no one hold me back! I shall drink of it and I shall live of it. Let me not be my own life! I lived evilly of myself; I have been death to myself; I come back to life in you. (XII.10)

Immediately, however, he feels reassured: "already, Lord, in my inner ear I have heard your voice loud and strong" (XII.11–12). He uses this phrase three times within two paragraphs, and repeatedly through the rest of the book, especially in an imaginary debate with the Manichaeans over the interpretation of Genesis (XII.15).

Perhaps he has chosen to discuss Genesis precisely in order to exorcise his continuing terror of the recollected self's potential for dissolution, for a "downward flow" that can only be arrested and given form by God's creative hand. He is fascinated by speculating on an intellectual "heaven of heavens, far above the heaven which we see," which is not susceptible to slippage. Although it is not co-eternal with God, . . . it clings to you without lapse and without cessation, suffers no vicissitude of time . . . and is neither altered by changing circumstances nor distracted into time" (XII.11). Here knowledge is nondiscursive; it is possible to know "in one act, not in part, not darkly, not through a glass, but as a whole, in manifestation, face to face." [35]

Woven into his meditation on the creation of the world are frequent expressions of longing for the stability of this "house of God": "Let me sigh toward you as I journey on my pilgrimage." Augustine has discovered a method for approaching immutability: "that which finds its happiness in always cleaving to God surpasses all extension and all the rolling space of time" (XII.15). The writing of the *Confessions* is itself an exercise in remembering and regathering, a methodical, discursive gathering of the "extension" that is his life into his resolution to cling to God, the

> chaste and strong delight, the solid joy and all good things unspeakable, all together at once, because you are the one supreme and true good. And I shall not turn aside until from this dispersed and deformed state of mine you gather all that I am into the peace of [Jerusalem], our dear mother. (XII.16)

In the final book of the *Confessions*, a different style from that of the narrative and philosophical books reveals a different agenda. Augustine's increased use of scriptural phrases, loosely woven together with commentary, makes the text dense, compacted, poetic. He undertakes a vast sorting of a complex group of paired opposites: the "heaven of heavens" and the "wavering watery darkness" of unformed matter; intelligible and sensible; unchangeableness and mutability; light and darkness; rising and falling; sight and faith; spiritual and material; fire and water; "death-dealing pleasures" and "life-giving pleasure." He is worried about "mixing" up the two entities in each pair. He reminds himself that in his sorting he must not extend the contrasting pairs to include good and evil, for "all things of your making are beautiful" (XIII.20). Nevertheless, it is of the utmost importance to him to "distinguish between the intelligible and the sensible" (XIII.18).

His topic is still the creation of the world, but his interest has shifted to the status of human life—this most volatile of all created entities. How did human life, the good creation of God, come to be the painfully ambiguous condition Augustine has experienced?

> If Adam had not slipped away from you, there would never have flowed from his womb the brackishness of that sea which is the human race, so deeply curious, so stormily tossing, so restlessly flowing here and there. (XIII.20)

Here Augustine's imagery of the squandered self is at its most vivid and poignant. Male and female bodies and generativity are conflated as he pictures Adam's slide away from God as a rush of briny liquid from his "womb" (*uterus*; XIII.20).[36] These "bitter waters" brought forth "the living soul" whose task it is to transcend its watery origin by "setting in order its affections by the strong force of continence" (XIII.34).

In this passage, the soul's out-flowing—its flowing away and down—is explicitly connected, in the figure of Adam, with the physical "flow" from male and female bodies by which reproduction occurs. I argued in chapter 3 that for Augustine, the body is not a metaphor for the psyche, but both are irreducibly interwoven, the one point at which Augustine cannot distinguish the spiritual and the sensible. Since it is at this point that intelligible and material—light and darkness—are most *mixed*, it is precisely here that continence must be practiced. Sexual intercourse continues to mix the soul, made in God's image (XIII.22), with the "wavering watery darkness" of formless matter which persists even after creation; sexual continence is, then, the decisive point at which a pivot can be accomplished, a return to God initiated, the hemorrhage arrested—in practice, if not in conceptual definition.

Augustine is tired of writing; he has explained enough: "Let the one who can, understand this. Let him ask guidance from you and not trouble me" (XIII.10). Yet he has not quite finished. His tale is of the past and the present; he has, to his satisfaction, scrutinized his past, defusing both its painful and its dangerously pleasurable memories. He has described his conversion, his days of leisure and philosophical discourse at Cassiciacum, his baptism. His autobiography is constantly and deeply shaped by the scripture he had studied intensively shortly after his appointment to the priesthood. Now he is a priest and bishop, a religious authority. It is this position he must still examine, and he does so in the final chapters of the *Confessions*. The ecclesiastical role he constructs for himself relates directly to his understanding of the present condition of the human race; the varieties of his ministerial duties relate directly to the return, the struggle back to the replenishing and refreshing source of being and pleasure.

God's ministers on earth have two duties: first, "by means of preaching and speaking . . . miracles and sacraments and mystic words" they must attract the attention of the ignorant. Fearing such mysterious signs, the ignorant will then investigate, because "ignorance is the mother of wonder" (XIII.21). The preacher or teacher must act as a mediator of "life-giving pleasures" to "unfaithful people" who have experienced only transitory pleasures. "The cause of the first preaching of the evangelists," Augustine says, was the unrestrained concupiscence of "souls who had their beginning from the earth." Like every good teacher, one of his greatest pleasures is learning:

And I heard you teaching me and commanding me. And I often do this. I find a delight in it, and whenever I can relax from my necessary duties I have recourse to this pleasure. . . . And sometimes working within me you open for me a door into a state of feeling which is quite unlike anything to which I am used—a kind of sweet delight, which, if I could only remain permanently in that state, would be something not of this world, not of this life. (X.40)

Delight, he knows, is communicable; it can be "caught" from a fine teacher or preacher.

In the *Confessions*, Augustine always discusses the sacraments as the entrance and initiation stage of the spiritual life.[37] In fact, it is his mention of sacraments and miracles as evidence of God's activity in the world that prompts Augustine to exclaim uneasily: "Can I be speaking untruly or mixing things up or failing to distinguish between the clear knowledge of these things in the firmament of heaven and the corporeal works in the wavy sea and under the firmament of heaven?" (XIII.20) Indeed, it is difficult to see how Augustine could understand the sacraments differently, embedded as they are in the staples of physical existence—water, bread, wine, oil. Augustine's literary and existential project was, as we have seen, defined as the practice of continence, in which attention and affection are withdrawn from the liquid darkness of the sensible world and placed in the fiery light and beauty of the spiritual world. How could he, at this point in his career, grant the sacraments a more significant role? His conclusion is that sacraments are necessary, but not sufficient:

> People are trained and initiated to accept the authority of corporeal sacraments, but they would never get beyond this point unless their souls became spiritually alive on another level and after the word of admission looked forward to perfection. (XIII.20; also XIII.34)

Clearly, however, Augustine is preoccupied with another aspect of his ministry; the third role he lists for pastors—after preaching and administering sacraments—is "to be a pattern to the faithful by living

among them and stirring them up to imitation"
(XIII.21). In particular, he sees the minister's role as
one of displaying the practice of continence in an actual human life, visible to everyone, because lived in
society. Souls become continent—not just sexually, but
in myriad ways—"by imitating those who imitate your
Christ" (XIII.21). Without the Mediator, Christ, whose
life on earth demonstrated the way to God through
continence, no one would have recognized the value
of this method, and living examples of continence—
mediations of a living practice—are still needed. Augustine knows well from his own experience the power
of example; he is quite prepared to recognize that responsibility and commit himself to it.

Finally, Augustine is a judge in the episcopal court
attached to his diocese: he sees his role there as involv-
ing judgments which combine justice, compassion,
and protection of the weak "from the grip of a powerful
oppressor" (XIII.17).

Religious authority is the next issue Augustine examines in relation to creation, concupiscence and continence, and ministry. It is a burning issue for him,
the reason he continues to write. He must "understand
by writing" his own position as an authority in the
church. Augustine begins by specifying the limits of
spiritual authority; even those who are most spiritual,
he insists, cannot judge which of the "unquiet and
restless people of this world . . . will come into the
sweetness of your grace and which will remain in per-
petual bitterness" (XIII.23).

Authority, he says, rightly belongs to the more spiritual, though all Christians, even those who have
barely made the beginning of a return to God, have

the capacity to "judge spiritually." His example of this ability is an interesting one:

> Not only those who are in spiritual authority but also those who are spiritually subordinate judge spiritually; for in this way, [God] made male and female in [God's] spiritual grace, where according to bodily sex there is neither male nor female. (XIII.23)

Nevertheless, having said this, Augustine will go on to associate the more and less spiritual with males and females respectively, in order to claim the authority of the first over the second. He thus undermines his own analogy's statement of the possibility of mutuality and interconnectedness. Equality of creation does not seem to him incompatible with a "natural" hierarchy:

> And just as in man's soul there is one part which rules by taking thought and another part which is subject to obedience, so for man also corporeally a woman was created to have a nature equal indeed to his in mind and rational intelligence, but to be in sex subjected to the masculine sex. (X.34)

At present, however, Augustine is concerned with his own authority. What does it consist of? How should it operate? On what is it based? He outlines the authority of the "spiritual man" not as power but as responsibility:

> He judges, approving what he finds good and condemning what he finds evil, and he exercises this judgment whether in the celebration of those sacraments by which are initiated those whom your mercy searches out . . . or in dealing with the significations and expres-

sions of words in interpreting, exposition, teaching, discussion, in praising you and praying to you. . . . The spiritual man also judges by approving what he finds good and condemning what he finds bad in the actions and way of life of the faithful, in their almsgiving . . . by the taming of the affections, in chastity, in fastings, in holy meditations; also of those things which are perceived by the bodily senses. Of all these things he is now said to judge, and in these things too he has the power to correct. (XIII.23)

Augustine's interlocking theory of authority is in place. He has sorted into hierarchically arranged pairs all the contrasting opposites he has found, from the "heaven of heavens" and unformed matter to soul and body, male and female. His theory of society will gradually come to be fitted into this scheme, reaching its clearest treatment twenty years later in the *City of God* (XIX.13–15).

Augustine was excited, satisfied, and pleasured by his textual contemplation, but is his reader? The reader he has attracted with the promise of a spicy autobiography is not likely to find philosophical musings as entertaining as a narrative of events and personalities. It is time to assess the textual gains and losses of the last four books of the *Confessions.*

Clearly, Augustine is still analyzing pleasure in these books. Now, however, it is "true pleasure," its source and its morphology, that he wants to understand, whereas in the earlier books he had examined the sources of transitory, and thus false, "pleasures." Augustine's deconstruction of his illusory pursuit of pleasures in books 1 to 9 is followed by a reconstruction in books 10 to 13. Yet there are profound differences between these two parts of the *Confessions*, differences that often strike first-time readers as so fundamental that they feel they are reading a different—and substantially less enchanting—book; frequently they do not continue to read into book 10. Augustine himself worried about retaining his reader's interest: "if my tongue and pen were to confess . . . all the knots that you untied for me on this question, which of my readers could hold out to take it all in?" (XII.6)

Furthermore, there is a new element of condescension toward his readers, imagined now as his congregation, in these books. He seldom pleads for sympathetic understanding. Rather, aware of his own authority, he assumes that he must "talk down" to most people: "How can we convey an idea of it to minds that are not very quick?" (XII.4) "Some people are used to thinking in material terms . . . such people are still feeble little animals" (XII.27). Yet "the writing of one who dispenses your word"—who can Augustine have in mind?—will, he believes, "do good to many who will preach and comment upon it, and from a narrow measure of speech it will spread and overflow into streams of liquid truth" (XII.27). The text, then, has a new, self-conscious responsibility. It must skillfully juggle the theoretical interests of the author with a concern for the reader's instruction.

How can the later books which treat such dense topics as the construction of subjectivity, memory, time, and creation claim to be a text of pleasure for author or reader? We have examined the devices by

which Augustine created, in the first nine books, a per-
meable text, a text to which the reader must react, a
text that evokes the reader's own experience, an invit-
ing text. By comparison, the last books are didactic;
they reason carefully; their pace is leisurely, but they
do not insist on the reader's co-authorship. They do
not invite rebuttal, counter explanation, or corro-
boration from the reader. They consider answers
rather than press desperate existential questions. The
contradictions of the earlier books have paled into par-
adoxes, no longer unsettling, rankling, disturbing.

Yet "the text of pleasure is not necessarily the text
that recounts pleasures."[38] And, as we have seen, some
of the objects Augustine had written about as false
pleasures—good in themselves, but failing to produce
happiness for their grasping lovers—reappear in the
closing books of the *Confessions* as real, re-formed
pleasures. At least one pleasure, however, is conspicu-
ously missing: Augustine did not integrate sexuality
into his reconstruction of true pleasure as he did, for
example, the pleasures of the senses. Yet, significantly,
poignantly, his understanding of the spiritual life itself
depends for its structure on the sexual activity he
has known. The spiritual life is defined by retaining,
collecting, rather than spilling and scattering, the
precious, dangerously fluid and slippery "self."
Augustine's sexuality "returns" as form rather than
content of his reformed life.

One of the great pleasures, for a reader, of the narrative books of the *Confessions* was their colorful
sketches of people. Compare, for example, Augustine's
treatment of the people of the first nine books with
those he mentions in the later books. The converted

Augustine relates several relationships in which, rather than seducing him to spill and squander himself, people help and support him in collecting and channeling himself: Alypius attends and participates in his conversion to chastity (VIII.12), and it was in conversation with Monica that Augustine enjoyed the experience of spiritual delight in which together they "just lightly touched" Wisdom (IX.10). These incidents, however, occur in the narrative books.

In books 10 to 13, shadowy people appear from time to time, primarily as adversaries. In book 12, for example, "they" dispute Augustine's admittedly tentative interpretations of Genesis. His interpretations are, in fact, framed against these opponents and what "they say." Indeed, the salient characteristic of the people mentioned is that they agree or disagree with Augustine. All are sketched in the briefest possible way, their ideas characterized—caricatured?—only as contrast to Augustine's: "those who hold these views are mad; they do not see your works by your spirit, nor do they recognize you in them" (XIII.30).

Augustine's views, though he often acknowledges that they lack scriptural support, are nevertheless right, whispered by God directly into his "inner ear." Furthermore, they carry the authority of a bishop's voice. Augustine and his views are not only converted, they are also institutionalized. He is sexually continent, not desiring that other people meet his sexual needs; he does, however, require that people accept his interpretation of Christian faith and scriptures. Perhaps the eagerness to establish his authority that shows so frequently in books 12 and 13 reflects his insecurity in a new position. His relationship with peo-

ple has changed profoundly. He now evidences an offi-
cial concern and affection for people—as preacher,
celebrant, bishop, judge, and, most importantly, as
model of continence. As with most powerful people, Augustine is not conscious of the power, but rather of the
pressures, the demands.

To his great credit, Augustine suspects and wor-
ries about his need for praise. He scrutinizes at length
his "wish to be feared and loved" (X.36). Apparently,
the primary way he elicits praise is his rhetorical skill
so it is this talent that must be controlled. Repeating
the exact words of his prayer for sexual continence,
Augustine begs: "Give what you command, and command what you will" (X.29). He refers to "continence of
the tongue." He confesses that "the tongue is the fur-
nace in which we are tried every day" (X.37). He is unsure of whether he has made any progress at all in
controlling his tongue. Reading himself in the best
possible light for the moment, he asks himself whether
he does not, perhaps, rejoice in praise because it demonstrates the good judgment of the person who praises
him? Sighing, he admits that when he is praised for a
certain quality, his joy in that quality is increased, as
he feels it should not be. In this matter, Augustine
finds it less easy to understand and assess himself
than in other matters:

> With regard to the pleasures of the flesh and the unnec-
> essary curiosity for knowledge I can see how far I have
> advanced in the ability to control my mind simply by
> observing myself when I am without these things. . . .
> For I can then ask myself how much or how little I mind
> not having them. (X.37)

Praise, however, is apparently never lacking, and "unless a thing is not there I cannot tell whether it is difficult or easy for me to be without it" (X.37). In the chapters in which Augustine examines his love of praise, he repeatedly acknowledges lack of self-knowledge: "I am in doubt . . . Whether this is really how I feel I do not know . . . I am troubled . . . I doubt myself. . .show me myself" (X.36–38). He concludes this uneasy discussion with his formulaic prayer for continence: "I pray that what is scattered in me may be brought together so that nothing of me may depart from you" (X.40).

The last books of the *Confessions* are, to me, profoundly sad. They construct a created order in which things (XIII.9) and people—especially, but not exclusively, women (XIII. 36)—have *places*. People no longer exhibit the delightful and confusing diversity, perversity, motility, unpredictability of the people with whom the young Augustine had searched for pleasures. In short, *no real people* appear in these books. The passionate, disorderly, rude, erotic, and colorful people of the earlier books have, in the last books, given way to shades with astral bodies, alluded to but not described. The vivid and tormented friendships in the narrative of Augustine's life, his relationships with real—and imperfect—parents, teachers, fellow students, and women, abruptly terminate as Augustine reconstructs people, beginning with his parents (IX.13), as "fellow pilgrims," without strong emotional affect for him.

Is the bleakness of Augustine's relationships in the

last books accidental? Is it incidental to his change of
style from autobiographical narration to philosophical
and theological essay? Or, does the change in style reflect and express a change in Augustine himself? Augustine would be the first to agree that this is the case;
indeed, the *Confessions* strives for this effect. Augustine skillfully juxtaposes a chaotic, painful, vivid
early life to an orderly, recollected, and service-oriented
Christian life. We should read books 10 to 13, then, *as*
autobiographical in the strictest sense, a continuation
of the earlier books' narration of who he is.[39] The textual disjunction—autobiographical narration to phil-
sophical essay—signals the disjunction Augustine
experienced and for which he seeks precise expression.

This *is* the converted, institutionalized Augustine—the new Augustine, anxious to demonstrate his
distance from the old Augustine. His readers, however, must find continuity within profound discontinu-
ity, as the continuity of address—God, the supportive
reader—suggests. Augustine's point is the mysterious
volatility of human life, particularly of human life that
God has undertaken to "remake." This is the same Augustine the reader has followed through confusion,
perplexity, compulsiveness, and passion to resolution,
understanding, peace. The losses—in the immediacy,
vividness, intensity of the text are profound, but these
are noticed only by the disobedient reader. The obedient reader will, as the text so insistently directs, notice
only the gains, the relief, the consistency, coherence,
organization of the last four books, a *systematic* exploration of memory, time, and creation. This exploration
is not passionless, but passion has been subordinated
to an order, the order of creation, beginning with "un-

formed matter." Just as God gave form to "unformed matter" in creation, so the middle-aged Augustine, with a deft hand and implacable eye, has formed the "unformed matter"—disorderly, concupiscent, poured out—of the young Augustine's life.

It may be helpful briefly to consider Augustine's alteration in twentieth-century terminology. The passion and energy of the young Augustine has been sublimated, gathered into the bishop's demanding duties. Sublimated passion effectively transmogrifies psychic energy, resisting its expenditure in one activity in order to invest it in a chosen project. The sublimation of sexual energy, Freud wrote, is necessary for the creation of civilization. In contrast to repression, in which psychic energy is expended in concealing from consciousness the repressed contents, sublimation transfers energy from one object to another *without loss*. This psychoanalytic model interestingly rewords Augustine's own model of concupiscence and continence.

Augustine's enormous literary corpus and his indefatigable work as pastor, bishop, and judge suggest that Augustine's sublimation—his transfer of psychic energy from concupiscence to continence, and its relocation in chosen projects—was, on one level, without loss. My interest, however, is not at present on Augustine's successful life, but on the successes and failure of his text. And, taking seriously and examining honestly my reaction, as well as the reported reactions of many other readers, to the final books of the *Confessions*, I must acknowledge that there is loss. True, instead of the young Augustine's acknowledged abuse of others, there is the pastor, caring for others, responsible for them, feeding them, and providing a model of continence for people for whom he feels enormous responsibility. Yet the older Augustine is better at judging others than at seeing their beauty. Recollected, and recollecting an abstract, contentless beauty—*pulchritudo tam antiqua et tam nova* (X.27)—Augustine finds *this* beauty normative. It is the "light" or lens through which everything else is filtered, a lens which selects, above all, order, peace, stability, rest. Beside this immaterial beauty the kaleidoscope of the rushing bright brief lifefulness of "creatures" pales into bleak presentiments of their inevitable death and dissolution.

For the author of the *Confessions* has, as the colloquial expression puts it, been burned. He has been frightened and damaged by the painful abrasiveness of his early experience. He insists now on loving only what he can love without fear of loss. "What madness it is not to know how to love people as they should be loved!" (IV.7) And to love without the risk—the certainty—of loss is to love only God. Let us understand Augustine carefully here: when one carries whatever—whomever—one loves to the place to which the "whole torrent of one's love flows," one sees others in the light of the timeless beauty of God. This great beauty does not dwarf or render insignificant the particular beauty of a person, but invests that person with a larger-than-life significance. To love the neighbor in God, Augustine claims, is to love the beauty of the soul rather than to lust after the body. Moreover, Augustine makes the startling claim that when one sees people "in God," it is God who sees them through one's "inner eye." Augustine claims not only that he can love by participation in God's love, but also that he can see as God sees. This "God's-eye view" validates Augustine's judgments of goodness and badness. The excruciating instability of judgment, insecurity of pronouncement, and indecision of the young Augustine are gone. Now Augustine can say repetitiously, "I know." He is always careful to specify the limits of the "I know," to mark these limits with "I do not know." Nevertheless, the "I do not know" has suddenly become the criteria by which he identifies the nonessential, unimportant, and marginal.

The reader, then "should" enjoy the last four books of the *Confessions* more than the first nine books. After all, they collect more inclusively and comprehensively; they evaluate more decisively and with greater assurance; they provide the reader with *conclusions*. Yet generation after generation of readers has taken more pleasure in the disorderly narration—full of asides, contradictions, variable address, disjunction, frustrating gaps and ommissions, interjection, ejaculation—of books 1 to 9 to the contemplative exposition of books 10 to 13.

Clearly, author's pleasure and reader's pleasure do not coincide. Augustine assures his reader that the "difficult labor and sweat" of writing the account of his youth are more painful and embarrassing than the confident theological speculation of the later books. Longing for peace, he is pleasured by finding its trustworthy source. Needing order, he takes pleasure in identifying the relative goodness of people and objects according to the order of their creation. Horrified of heresy, he finds joy in God's confirmation of his views in his inner ear. Yet the *Confessions* does not reproduce Augustine's pleasure in his reader.

Although I have argued that the later books are autobiographical in the sense that they accurately reflect Augustine's mature preoccupations, lifestyle, and fascinations, they do not narrate people and events. Thus they present a more oblique, less accessible auto-biography. More and more of what Augustine wants to communicate can be put in scriptural language that precedes and absorbs individual experience. This is a language that does not evoke personal experience, that tacitly declines to elicit a reader's assent or objection. Less engaged, the reader is less pleasured.

Moreover, in books 10 to 13, Augustine's body, for-merly so persistently present, so textually fleshed out, is in hiding. It is not absent, but subordinated and sublimated. Absent as desire, sense, and pleasure, the body is present as support system, servant, and con-stant reminder of fragility and vulnerability: "we were sometimes darkness, and we bear about with us relics of this darkness in our body" (XIII.14). The young Au-gustine's sexual body—insistent, demanding, aggres-sive—is present in the later books only in diluted, emaciated, furtive form, as wet dream, hastily expelled from Augustine's "real self." The docile body of the con-templative books knows its place as ancillary, meta-phor of the triumphant soul—as flesh made word.

The reader's pleasure in the narrative autobiogra-phy, viewed from the perspective of the contemplative books is itself perverse, concupiscent. The orderly ex-position of the last four books of the *Confessions* re-quires that the reader receive more pleasure from order than from chaos, more pleasure from confidence than from insecurity, more pleasure from peace than from frenzy. If she resists this seduction, she will notice a dramatic diminution of textual pleasure. She may even experience textual harassment in the demand that she act as passive listener to Augustine's reiteration of his satisfaction rather than as the active voyeur she was in the narrative books. Augustine had described the autobiographical narration of the earlier books as "difficult ground, not to be worked without much hard labor." In the last books of the *Confessions*, it is the *reader* who must plough through some difficult ground.

Despite the reader's reversal of the author's pleasure, Augustine declares himself successful in his "text of pleasure." He has, he says, managed both to find maximal pleasure that is permanent, and to "save" sensory delights by embedding them in the great beauty. He has dismantled or unraveled "false" pleasure—pleasure diluted with pain, undermined by evanescence, constructed by lack. And he has identified "true" pleasure, pleasure that is secure, guaranteed, undiluted, everlasting. He feels that he has recovered the "true" senses, salvaging their transitory delights by placing them in a permanent object:

But what do I love when I love you? Not the beauty of the body nor the glory of time, not the brightness of light shining so friendly to the eye, not the sweet and various melodies of singing, not the fragrance of flowers and ungents and spices, not manna and honey, not limbs welcome to the embraces of the flesh: it is not these that I love when I love my God. And yet, I do love a kind of light, melody, fragrance, food, embracement when I love my God; for he is the light, the melody, the fragrance, the food, the embracement of my inner self— there where is a brilliance that space cannot contain, a sound that time cannot carry away, a perfume that no breeze disperses, a taste undiminished by eating, a

clinging together that no satiety will sunder. This is
what I love when I love my God. (X.6)

Augustine also claims to have recovered the body,
now redeemed from socialization and tucked firmly
into the soul as its partner or tool. The narrative autobiography had recognized the soul *in* the body and its
movements, meticulously, relentlessly observing the
somatic effects of psychic states. Recall, for example,
Augustine's "dear friend" who was baptized while lying
unconscious and at the point of death. Upon his recovery, the unregenerate Augustine joked with him
about the baptism, thinking his friend will join read-
ily in making fun of the ritual. Instead, his friend admonished him with a "confident authority," assuring
Augustine that the baptism administered to his unconscious body had taken effect in his psyche (IV.4).
Remember also the violent physical movements with
which Augustine's conversion of the body to continence occurred (VIII.12). Recall a hundred incidents in
which the movements of the body signaled and spec-
ified movements of the soul. In the last four books of
the *Confessions*, Augustine no longer painstakingly
observes his body in order to understand what goes on
in his soul.

Formerly the soul's "helpless victim," used and
damaged in the pursuit of sex, power, and possessions,
the docile body is still the mark of the soul's hegemony.
There is gain, in that the body is no longer required to
bear the destructive burden of the soul's concupiscence; there is also loss, revealed in Augustine's definition of body as subordinate, obedient. Augustine's
formula is: "If bodies please you, praise God for them

and turn your love back from them to their maker, lest you should displease him in being pleased by them" (IV.12). Order has been achieved; the body is in its place.

A body tends to go of its own weight to its own place. Fire tends to rise upward; a stone falls downward. Things are moved by their own weights and go toward their proper places. If you put oil underneath water it will rise above the level of the water; if you pour water on top of oil, it will sink below the oil; things are moved by their own weights and go to their proper places. When at all out of their place, they become restless; put them back in order and they will be at rest. My weight is my love; wherever I am carried, it is my love that carries me there. By your gift we are set on fire and are carried upward; we are inflamed and we go. (XIII.9)

I have discussed the losses, for a reader—for *this* reader—in books 10 to 13. It is only fair to let Augustine have the last word. What are the gains? Hierarchical order—everything in its place—has overcome the chaos in which the objects of lust restlessly butt against and displace each other, vying for priority—a sort of Brownian movement in the soul. It also resolves the contradiction between infinite desire and unsatisfying—because finite—objects. Augustine claims to have found order by crossing through disorder, comfort through exploring discomfort. Order, he has discovered, can be incorporated, incarnated, in the continent body.

The mark of true order, order that accurately reflects the relative value of created entities, is effortless spontaneity: "things are moved by their own weights and go to their proper places." The "place" of human beings is determined by the object toward which the "whole torrent" of their love rushes, on whether that love is "spilled and scattered" on objects in the world or collected, returned to the source of being, the great beauty. Instead of having the consistency of messily spilled and scattered muddy liquid, a human being can, by God's gift, become flame, caught up into the life of the spirit, with a gasp of pleasure: *inardescimus et imus.*

Epilogue

The *Confessions*, I have endeavored to demonstrate, is a text of pleasure. It recounts pleasures, but more importantly, its central problematic is how to find, get, and keep maximal pleasure. As a "great text of the Western world," it has also played a role in the social construction of desire. This powerful statement of human desire and fulfillment has informed Western people's amorphous, polymorphous, multiple and inarticulate longings. Augustine's experience has shown that articulations of desire and fulfillment are fundamentally important in generating, provoking, and forming individual desire.

Moreover, "human" desire is always marked by the particularities of individual lives, by socially constructed gender assumptions, expectations, and roles, by social location, institutional affiliation, class, and race. If the claim that desire is socially constructed and differentiated according to these factors seems far-fetched, attempt to imagine the protagonist of the *Confessions* as a woman. Could Augustine's demanding, energetic, aggressive passion have occurred—much less been admired and become a classic—in a woman, in his time or ours?

I am envious of the social construction and support of Augustine's passion, both his relentless pursuit of worldly satisfaction and his latter passionate love of God, combined with institutional authority. To search frantically, desperately; to long restlessly, lustfully, feverishly; to embody the kind of consuming and complex desire that knows its object when it touches it . . . few women have sustained such uncompromising desire, at least partly because women have had few literary paradigms, few images, few models.[40] Rather, in the societies of the Christian West, women's desire has been constructed to serve male desire as its mirror and counterpart.

The lack of female models does not mean, of course, that no women have managed to formulate and pursue a distinctive desire; it does mean that it is immensely more difficult for women to do so in societies that have no female epic heroes, no models but male models for passionately seeking women. Many—though not most—women have learned to use male models, to adopt, adapt, or rebel against these models of heroic hunger. Educated women have learned to read as men, blind to the biology and socialization, the institutions, and the legal and social arrangements that have *authorized* the author.

This has been, until recently, my own unacknowledged strategy for getting what I need from Western culture in order to imagine and understand my life. Until the summer of 1989, I always read the *Confessions* as a man—or, perhaps, rather, as that bodyless, fleshless, neutered "human being" that exists nowhere but was required by my education. I have been seduced, enchanted, ravished by this text. Augustine's autobiography remains for me crucial evidence that approaching the world with life and mettle and vigor and passion—even when most misguided—leads one by the most direct possible route to the Great Beauty. It is not an exaggeration to acknowledge that reading Augustine has altered the course of my life and that I continue to be profoundly grateful for his authorship.

Yet I am a woman, and I notice in the *Confessions* who speaks and who listens; I detect the myriad ways that the male author's experience informs and gives body to his text. And I wonder if there might not be more fruitful metaphors for the spiritual life than male sexual continence, collecting and retaining "precious bodily fluids." I wonder why alternative metaphors and images are so difficult to find and why, when images relating to the female body are suggested, they often seem self-conscious, reactionary, and awkward. Why is there no metaphor drawn from female experience that connotes "ground-breaking" generativity and productivity as does the word *seminal*?

It is certainly significant that Augustine critiqued his society's construction of male sexuality, equating tumescence and the myth of male helplessness in the face of sexual urges with pride and sin. He experienced, he says, a vast relief and freedom in the practice of continence. Later in his career he formulated a model of sexuality based on principles of complementarity and responsibility. It was not a model he had ever lived, and it did not go as far as to imagine equality and mutuality, but it became an enormously influential model. Without the institutional and personal authority of an Augustine, no alternative model could hope to produce the social effects of Augustine's formulation of heterosexual relationship.

Clearly, Augustine failed to address gender assumptions planted deeply in his society and in his own psyche. Rather, the *effect*, even if not the intention, of his authorship was to reinforce rather than to alter Western gender constructions by giving theological validation to beliefs about women's and men's "natures". A female-gendered reading of Augustine is often, then, a ravaging—rather than a ravishing—experience. In my reading of the *Confessions* I have endeavored to acknowledge and describe both its dangers and its delights. It is, I think, necessary to see both in full strength in order to understand either. Having seen both with clarity and vividness, I can take up Augustine's task of strenuous critique and reconstruction rather than his conclusions. I can learn from his longing to *have it all* rather than from his own resolution. I can relish the strength and beauty and richness of his repertoire of metaphors and images without relinquishing my questions, my sensitivities, my reservations, and my images. And I can allow Augustine's intense vision of the Great Beauty to alert me to its presence—a presence Augustine himself saw as above the vicissitudes of human life—*within* the sensuous sensible world, in human relationships, and in passionate longing in its myriad beautiful and unbeautiful forms.

Notes

1. *Confessions* XIII.9; frequent references to the *Confessions* throughout the text follow this form. English translations are based on Rex Warner, *The Confessions of St. Augustine* (New York: New American Library, 1963); I have frequently changed the translation when the Latin supported a more literal or vivid word or phrase.

2. See "Infancy, Parenting and Nourishment in Augustine's *Confessions*," *Journal of the American Academy of Religion*, September 1982.

3. See *Augustine on the Body* (Missoula, Montana: Scholars Press, 1979).

4. See *Fullness of Life: Historical Foundations for a New Asceticism* (Westminster Press, 1981), chap. 3.

5. *Confessions* IX. 2.

6. "Vision: The Eye of the Body and the Eye of the Mind in St. Augustine's *De trinitate* and the *Confessions*," *Journal of Religion*, April 1983, and *Practicing Christianity: Critical Perspectives for an Embodied Spirituality* (New York: Crossroad, 1988).

7. Roland Barthes, *Le plaisir du texte*; English trans. *The Pleasure of the Text*, trans. Richard Miller (New York: Hill and Wang, 1975).

8. *De anima* 1A. 1. 403a. 15.

9. Rainer Maria Rilke, *Duino Elegies* X: "und wir, die an steigendes Glück/denken, empfänden die Rührung,/die uns beinah bestürzt,/wenn ein Glückliches *fällt.*"

10. *Disorder and Early Sorrow* is the title of a short story by Thomas Mann, in *Death in Venice and Seven Other Stories* (New York: Vintage, 1963).

11. *Confessions* IV.11.

139

12. Barthes, *The Pleasure of the Text*, 55.

13. Ibid., 23.

14. James Salter, *Light Years* (San Francisco: North Point Press, 1982), 161.

15. Annette Kuhn, "The Body and Cinema: Some Problems for Feminism," in *Grafts: Feminist Cultural Criticism*, ed. Susan Sheridan (New York: Verso, 1988), 22.

16. Compare Luther's hermeneutical principle: "For when a man does not take his subject seriously and feels no personal interest in it, never has his heart in it and finds it wearisome, chilling, or nauseating, how can he help saying absurd, inept, and contradictory things all the time, since he conducts the case like one drunk or asleep, belching out between his snores, 'Yes, No,' as different voices fall on his ears? . . .theology requires such feeling as will make a man vigilant, penetrating, intent, astute, and determined." *The Bondage of the Will*, in *Luther and Erasmus: Free Will and Salvation*, trans. E. Gordon Rupp and Philip S. Watson (Philadelphia: Westminster Press, 1969), 179.

17. *Retractationes* II.6.

18. *rapio*: the verb carries connotations of violence.

19. The Council of Calcedon in A.D. 451, fifty years after Augustine's *Confessions*, decided on a definition of belief in the full humanity and full divinity of Christ.

20. As Thomas Traherne said twelve hundred years later, "We love we know not what, and therefore everything allures us." *Centuries of Meditation*, ed. Bertram Dobell (London: n.p., 1908), 3.

21. In 426–27, when he wrote the last book of *De doctrina christiana*, Augustine acknowledged the importance of rhetorical skill: "Who would dare to say that truth should stand in the person of its defenders unarmed against lying, so that they who wish to urge falsehoods may know how to make their listeners benevolent or attentive or docile in their presentation, while the defenders of truth are ignorant of that art? Should [the defenders of falsehood] speak briefly, clearly, and plausibly while the defenders of truth speak so that they tire their listeners, make themselves difficult to understand and what they have to say dubious? . . . Should [the defenders of falsehood], urging the minds of their listeners into error, ardently exhort them, moving them by speech so that they terrify, sadden, and exhilarate them, while the defenders of truth are sluggish, cold, and somnolent? Who is so foolish as to think this to be wisdom? While the faculty of eloquence, which is of great value in urging either evil or justice, is in itself indifferent, why

should it not be obtained for the uses of the good in the service of truth if the evil usurp it for the winning of perverse and vain causes in defense of iniquity and error?" (IV. 2).

22. *Confessions* IX.1.

23. Eileen O'Neill, "(Re)presentations of Eros: Exploring Female Sexual Agency," in *Gender/Body/Knowledge*, ed. Alison M. Jagger and Susan R. Bordo (New Brunswick, N.J.: Rutgers University Press, 1989), 70.

24. Audre Lorde, *Sister Outsider* (Freedom, Calif.: Crossing Press), 57.

25. Elizabeth Spelman and others have recently criticized the claim that one can read, think, or write "as a woman" on the grounds that this locution masks the enormous differences among and between women. I recognize the validity of this criticism and acknowledge that it is unjust and deeply problematic for white feminists to assume that they can speak for all women. My claim, then, is not that I can read as *a*—meaning *any*—woman, but that I read as *one* woman, formed and informed nonetheless by experiences common to many North American women. *Inessential Woman: Problems of Exclusion in Feminist Thought* (Boston: Beacon Press, 1990).

26. For a discussion of representations of the female body, see Margaret R. Miles, *Carnal Knowing: Female Nakedness and Religious Meaning in the Christian West* (Boston: Beacon Press, 1989), 22

27. *Gender/Body/Knowledge*, 70.

28. James Hillman, *Myth of Analysis* (Evanston, Ill.: Northwestern University Press, 1972), 141. I am grateful to Professor David Miller of Syracuse University for this citation.

29. *Epistula* ccxxxi.6.

30. Clarissa W. Atkinson has demonstrated that the figure of Monica was an important model for the social construction of motherhood for more than a thousand years, and with effects that reach to our own time. *The Oldest Vocation: Christian Motherhood in the Middle Ages* (Ithaca, N.Y.: Cornell University Press, 1991).

31. The words here translated "drunkenness" and "intoxication" are the same Latin word: *inebrio*.

32. Geoffrey Galt Harpham named and discussed the dynamic of temptation and resistance in a remarkable book, *The Ascetic Imperative in Culture and Criticism* (Chicago: University of Chicago Press, 1987).

33. Augustine, *De musica* VI. 11. 29.

34. *Confessions* XIII.27.

35. 1 Corinthians 13:12 is the second most frequently quoted scriptural verse in the *Confessions*. The most frequently quoted verse is Romans 1:20: "Ever since the creation of the world his invisible nature . . . has been clearly perceived in the things that have been made."

36. The Cambridge Patristic Texts edition of the *Confessions* notes that this conflation of male and female reproductive organs is "a remarkable example of catachresis," adding that "it is to be explained, no doubt, by the fact that 'Adam' is used generically rather than personally"; this interpretation misses the point that since it is the male body and male sexual experience that structures the text, it is startling to find Augustine suddenly grafting a female reproductive organ onto a male body. *The Confessions of Augustine*, ed. John Gibb and William Montgomery (Cambridge: Cambridge University Press, 1908), 428, n. 9.

37. Augustine narrated his baptism in one sentence, in striking contrast to the lengthy painstaking description of his conversion to continence (IX.6; see also XIII.34).

38. Barthes, *The Pleasure of the Text*, 55.

39. Augustine remarks of the *Confessions*: "There believe what is said of me, not by others, but by myself . . . there mark me, and see what I have been in myself, by myself" (*Epistula* ccxxxi.6).

40. Teresa De Lauretis comments on "the weakness of female desire, its reticence to expose itself, its lack of symbolic authorization." "The Essence of Triangle, or Taking the Risk of Essentialism Seriously: Feminist Theory in Italy, the U.S., and Britain," *Differences: A Journal of Feminist Critical Studies* 1, no. 2 (Summer 1989): 22.

Index